The Essence of Management Creativity

TONY PROCTOR
University of Keele

Prentice Hall

London   New York   Toronto   Sydney   Tokyo   Singapore
Madrid   Mexico City   Munich

First published 1995 by
Prentice Hall International (UK) Limited
Campus 400, Maylands Avenue
Hemel Hempstead
Hertfordshire, HP2 7EZ
A division of
Simon & Schuster International Group

© Prentice Hall International (UK) Ltd, 1995

Typeset in 10/12pt Palatino
by Keyset Composition, Colchester, Essex

Printed and bound in Great Britain by
T. J. Press (Padstow) Ltd, Padstow, Cornwall

Library of Congress Cataloging-in-Publication Data

Proctor, Tony.
    The essence of management creativity/by Tony Proctor
      p.   cm.
    Includes bibliographical references and index.
    ISBN 0-13-356536-X
    1. Group problem solving. 2. Brainstorming. 3. Creative thinking.
    4. Creative ability in business. I. Title.
    HD30.29.P764 1995
    658.4'094—dc20
                                     95–12260
                                         CIP

British Library Cataloguing in Publication Data

A catalogue record for this book is available from
the British Library

ISBN 0-13-356536-X

1 2 3 4 5   99 98 97 96 95

Contents

v

Preface

Management Creativity is an old well-established topic but at the same time, as a subject area in its own right it is relatively new. I was introduced to the subject by Tudor Rickards in 1984–5 while I was a doctoral researcher at Manchester Business School. I was extremely intrigued by the subject and although my key interests at the time were Marketing and Business Computing I decided to show more than a passing interest in the subject.

In the late 1980s I was interested in computer assisted creativity and, indeed, my doctoral thesis addressed this particular aspect of creativity. Few people prior to this had addressed the subject and I became somewhat of a pioneer. Perhaps it was the initial pioneering spirit that eventually led me to become engrossed in the subject of management creativity and, eventually, to produce this book.

When I moved to Keele University in 1987 it was to develop Marketing as a subject within the curriculum. This I did, but at the same time I began to run undergraduate and postgraduate options in Management Creativity. I can only say that I was extremely surprised by the great amount of interest that was shown in the subject. It became one of the most popular options available.

Before writing this book I had been conscious for some time that there was not really a suitable textbook to use for the courses I was running. With this in mind I decided to write the book. It covers most of the material one would expect to find in a book on creative problem solving for management. Arguably, there is other material which could have been included. However, I feel that the material I have included forms a tight entity in its own right and to include material which might equally well be considered under the heading of such subjects as the management of change or innovation would not be appropriate.

Creativity and Management Creativity can encompass a wide spectrum of material. What I have included here is essentially concerned with creative problem solving. It contains many practical techniques and methods which will appeal to students and to practising managers alike.

1

Creativity in management

This book is about creativity and problem solving in management. Many management problems require creative insights in order to find satisfactory solutions to them. Dreaming up new product ideas to gain an advantage over competitors in the market-place is an example. This first chapter introduces creative thinking and explores its importance in management problem solving. An overview of creative problem-solving techniques and methods is then presented within the general framework of problem-solving strategy. The chapter introduces the reader to the different topics to be found in the individual chapters that follow.

Nature of creative thinking

Creativity is something that one comes across every day. One hears of creative people, admires creative objects of art or reads creative books. Yet despite our ability to recognize creativity manifesting itself, there is considerable confusion about what creativity really is.

Wertheimer (1945) suggested that creative thinking involved breaking down and restructuring our knowledge about a phenomenon in order to gain new insights into its nature. Understanding how we see things may therefore have considerable influence on our ability to think creatively. Kelly (1955) and Rogers (1954) both maintained that we can be creative by gaining an insight into our own understanding of a subject. Creativity occurs when we organize our thoughts in a way that leads readily to a different understanding of a situation.

The importance of creativity in management

The rapid growth of competition in business and industry is often given as a reason for wanting to understand more about the creative process (see, for example, Van Gundy, 1987). Many firms experience pressure to enhance old systems and products continually. Growth and survival can be related directly to an organization's ability to produce (or adopt) and implement new products or services and processes (Van Gundy, 1987); managers also need to discover new and better ways to solve problems (Ackoff and Vegara, 1988). In particular, an increasing number of problems have few or no precedents, hence there are fewer tried and tested ways of approaching them with the anticipation of reaching a successful outcome.

Trying to solve problems in the same way that they have always been solved in the past can sometimes lead to unforeseen difficulties and what may seem to be insurmountable barriers. This is particularly the case in a business environment which is experiencing rapid cultural, economic or technological change. Change is an ever-present phenomenon to which businesses of all kinds are forced to respond, if they want to stand the best chance of survival and prosperity.

It has been suggested that possessing creative ability is an essential asset for any leader (see, for example, Bennis and Nanus, 1985 and empirical evidence provided by Ekvall and Parnes, 1988). Creative leaders hunt actively for new problems and are especially successful in handling new challenges that demand solutions outside the routine of orthodox strategies. They often possess significant vision and are able to inspire others by their creative talents. Creativity is an important human resource and all organizations have to try to make use of this resource by devising settings in which creative talents are permitted to thrive.

There is evidence to support a direct link between creative thinking and organizational efficiency and effectiveness (for example, Raudsepp, 1987). Creativity also helps to improve the solutions to persistent organizational problems and has a broader role to play in an organization, since it helps to encourage profitable innovations, rekindles employee motivation and improves personal skills and team performance. Creativity is particularly important in marketing and corporate strategy formulation. A continuous flow of ideas for new products and services, and for improving work processes, provides the platform upon which an organization can develop its competitive advantage.

Despite the need for creativity in organizations many factors work against it (Figure 1.1). Van Gundy (1992) pointed out the kinds of factors involved. Managements, he argued, often believe that acquiring new technology through merger will spur innovation but, as he pointed out,

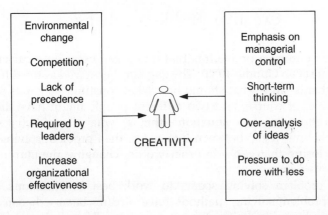

| Factors pushing for creativity | Factors pushing against creativity |

Figure 1.1 Some of the factors that push for creativity and some that push against it in organizations.

merged companies are not always compatible and this stifles innovation. Emphasis on managerial control, short-range thinking and over-analysis of new ideas often lead to creativity not having a chance to succeed. Among other reasons cited by Van Gundy were pressure to do more with less and perceptions that creative people are born and not made. Budget constraints make it difficult for companies to innovate. Zero-based budgets, personnel cutbacks and reduced product–cycle times all make it difficult to increase innovation. There is also a prevailing attitude among many managers that creativity is something that cannot be learned.

While many managers may think that creativity cannot be developed, Van Gundy indicated that creativity training has increased in US companies from around 4 per cent of companies in 1985 to more than 26 per cent by 1989. He also commented that a study by the American Society for Training and Development reported that 31 per cent of US companies planned to offer creativity training during the next 3 years. There are no comparable figures for the United Kingdom but it would seem that the need for creativity training cannot be less than it is in the United States.

The need for creativity makes itself felt in most aspects of organizational decision making. New ideas are required and old ideas need to be re-examined. Creativity is the process of revealing, selecting, swapping around and combining one's store of facts, ideas and skills. Rickards (1988) described creativity as an 'escape from mental stuckness', an operational definition very much in keeping with its role in decision making and problem solving.

Creative problem solving

One way of defining a problem is that it is a gap between a current and a desired state (Van Gundy, 1988). The gap may be viewed as the difference between 'what is' and 'what should be'. What constitutes a gap is relative and subjective, of course, and two different people might have different perceptions about the same situation – that is, 'what is' and 'what should be'. If a problem is a gap between two states, then problem solving is the process of closing that gap – in other words, changing the current state into the desired one.

Creative problem solving seems to work best in situations where traditional problem-solving methods have already been exhausted. For well-structured problems, routine or ready-made solutions are well known. In such cases one usually has a pretty good idea about the problem states and how to transform the current state into the desired state. For example, suppose the problem is to explain why the money in the cash till of a shop at the end of the day does not equate with the difference between the initial float money and the receipts and refunds which have been issued during a day's trading. The current state and the desired state can easily be defined and clearly there can be several explanations for the discrepancy. Such a problem does not require creative problem-solving methods to find a solution.

Other problems, however, are not solved so easily. These problems have much less information available about them and are more ill-structured in nature. In these cases there is ambiguity about the problem states or how to transform the current state into the desired state. To solve such problems requires divergent thinking – that is, one needs to think of many different potential solutions. A problem faced by many managers, for example, concerns how to make the best use of their time. In such a case both the current and desired states may be difficult to define precisely and the method of effecting a transformation between the two states may be even less obvious.

The background of creative problem solving

Osborn (1957) proposed that creative thinking involved three stages:

☐ fact finding;
☐ idea finding; and
☐ solution finding.

Fact finding, he argued, contained two substages: problem definition and preparation. Problem definition is quite clearly an imperative. Not only is it the case that ill-structured problems are characterized by vague notions about the 'current and desired states' concerning the problem, but it would also be pointless to try to find solutions to problems that are ill-defined. Idea finding helps to generate potential ideas, and solution finding helps to evaluate and select the best ideas.

Osborn also noted that the more ideas generated, the greater the probability that a high quality solution will result. He also suggested that judgement should be deferred during idea generating. He felt that if the latter is not done, one can focus too much on evaluation and limit the total number of ideas. Separating the processes also helps to encourage a climate more conducive to creative ideas.

Another person to make a substantial impact on our thinking about creative problem solving (CPS) was psychologist Sydney J. Parnes. He conducted several major research studies on CPS and added new stages – problem finding and acceptance finding – which placed greater emphasis on problem definition and solution implementation. Parnes also suggested that each stage in the process should begin with a divergent search for data (without trying to evaluate it) and conclude with a convergent selection of the most important data.

The Osborn–Parnes model was refined further by Scott Isaksen and Donald Treffinger (1985). They added a preliminary problem-solving stage: objective finding. This stage helps identify a target area to resolve (i.e. the primary concern, challenge or opportunity).

Overview of the creative problem-solving process

Current thinking argues that the creative problem-solving process involves six stages, although it is not necessary to go through all the stages for every problem (Figure 1.2). Sometimes, for instance, one may begin at the problem-finding or idea-finding stage, depending on how much information is available and how much time is available. Whatever the case, however, the ground rule is to defer judgement. Data should always be listed and studied before it is evaluated.

Creative thinking comprises two kinds of thought process: *divergent* and *convergent* (see for example, Guilford, 1967). Divergent thinking develops and broadens out the thought process. Thinking divergently entails starting with a specific problem or idea and generating various perspectives on it. The purpose of divergent thinking is to ignore constraints and entertain all kinds of possibilities. Convergent thinking follows divergent thinking and it acts to narrow down the options available in order to obtain a number of satisfactory solutions to a problem or decision. When thinking

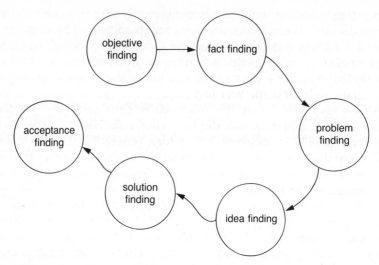

Figure 1.2   Six stages of the creative problem-solving process.

convergently, one begins with a wide perspective on a problem and proceeds to narrow down the focus to specific issues or options (Figure 1.3).

Each stage in the creative problem-solving process contains a set of divergent and convergent activities. That is, there is an initial search for data and then a narrowing down of the data. During the convergence one looks for material which is either very close to the point at issue or close enough to warrant further consideration.

Most consideration is given to 'hits': specific items that are identified as important or relevant to a particular stage (the best objectives during objective finding, the best facts during fact finding, etc.). 'Hotspots' is the name given to clusters of 'hits' which seem to be related to one another in some way. The six stages are discussed below.

Objective finding

At this stage one needs to target a problem area, beginning by using divergent thinking to generate a list of all the problems one is facing. Next one converges, identifying the most relevant problem area for further exploration. To facilitate, the problem is stated using the format:

'In what ways might we (I) do something or other?'

For example,

'In what ways might we reduce our marketing expenses?'

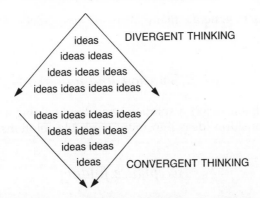

Figure 1.3 Divergent versus convergent thinking.

Before moving on to the next stage one needs to have identified the important problems (hits) and the key problem area or areas (hotspots). Here the criteria are applied:

☐ ownership (is one motivated to solve it?);
☐ priority (how important is the problem?); and
☐ critical nature (how urgent is it to solve this problem?).

Hopefully, by the end of this stage one should have identified the central problem or problems upon which to work.

Fact finding

This stage increases overall comprehension of the problem: the objective is to collect all the information related to the problem. This, in turn, helps to generate unique ideas. Convergence during this stage can again be assisted by using hits and hotspots. Fact finding helps to collect relevant data and may even enable one to see the previously identified problem or problems from a new perspective.

Problem finding

This stage uses fact-finding hits to develop the most productive problem definition possible.

Idea finding

The fourth stage in the creative problem-solving process helps to structure the search for potential solutions. The primary divergent activity during idea finding is to generate many ideas using a variety of idea-generation aids.

Solution finding

This stage helps to select a solution capable of solving a problem. It can be used to transform ideas into more workable solutions.

Acceptance finding

The last stage of the creative problem-solving process helps to implement a solution successfully. Major divergent activities involve:

1. listing potential implementation obstacles and ways to overcome them;
2. developing both preventive actions and contingency plans; and
3. generating an action plan to implement a solution.

An IDEAL model for problem solving

Bransford and Stein (1993) proposed a model for improving problem-solving skills. It is based on research in the field of problem solving by such people as Wertheimer (1945), Polya (1957) and Newell and Simon (1972). The components of the approach are represented by the acronym IDEAL, where:

I = Identify problems and opportunities
D = Define goals
E = Explore possible strategies
A = Anticipate outcomes and act
L = Look back and learn

The various stages in the model are explained below.

Identify problems and opportunities

Potential problems should be identified and treated as opportunities to do something creative. It is just as important to look for problems actively as it is simply to respond to them when they become critical or when they are noticed.

Defining goals

Different goals often reflect how people understand a problem. For example, the problem of a lack of strategic direction in a business could be identified. All concerned might agree that it could represent an opportunity to do something creative. However, there could be disagreement on what the goals should be. Some people might argue that the objective of the business should be growth into international markets, while others might argue for concentrating on making the business more profitable in domestic markets. In these two instances the goals reflect clearly how different groups perceive the same problem. Defining the goal is thus a crucial step in moving towards a solution to a problem.

Exploring possible strategies

This can involve re-analyzing the goals and considering options or strategies that might be employed to achieve those goals. For many problems it is easy to consider all the relevant information without experiencing a strain on short-term memory capacity. As problems increase in complexity this becomes more difficult to do. Experienced problem solvers often keep track of information by creating external representations. Rather than trying to keep all the information in their heads they write it down on paper – or use some other medium. This enables them to think more freely about the problem they want to solve. The benefits of doing this are obvious, really – try finding the sum of the first five prime numbers which are greater than 100 in your head! There are many ways of recording and analyzing a problem – graphs and Venn diagrams are examples. The most effective way to represent information depends on the nature of the problem. It has been noted by Hayes (1989) and Halpern (1989) that some problems are solved more readily if one uses verbal representation whereas others may be better represented visually or even mathematically. Other additional general approaches can include working a problem backward, or focusing on a simpler, specific situation – building scale models or performing experiments that simulate certain characteristics of a real world environment are good examples.

Although there are general strategies for solving problems, specialized knowledge is often necessary to solve some problems.

Anticipate outcomes and act

Once a strategy is selected, it is important to anticipate possible outcomes and then act on that strategy. In many situations an active role in testing strategies has to be taken before possible outcomes can be anticipated. The building and testing of a prototype can often help to anticipate the outcomes of particular strategies.

Look and learn

The last stage of the IDEAL model is to look at the effects of the particular strategy and learn from the experience: unfortunately, something which is quite often overlooked. When trying to solve a problem the emphasis should be on finding the *first* step rather than trying to find a complete solution immediately. Having tried out the first step and learned from the experience one can then proceed to work through subsequent steps. Test marketing is a case in point, where the launch of a new product is done on a gradual basis. Any aspects of the introduction that are less than satisfactory are corrected before the next stage in the roll-out process. Writing and debugging computer programs follow a similar process.

IDEAL framework and the creative process

The capacity to identify problems and opportunities is one of the most important steps in the creative process and the act of defining and redefining one's goals is a particularly important part of this process. Different goals suggest different lines of thought and have a powerful effect on the solution strategies that are considered. The 'anticipate and act' phase of the IDEAL model can help us to uncover inappropriate assumptions that may be limiting the creativity of our thinking. Long-term efforts to enhance creativity will not be successful unless one looks at the effects of one's actions and tries to learn from them (Figure 1.4).

The IDEAL problem-solving process is both complementary and supplementary to the creative problem-solving process.

How creative thinking may be used in management

Creative thinking benefits all areas and activities of management. It is required to find improved ways of marketing goods, to devise new

Stages in the creative problem-solving process	Stages in the IDEAL problem-solving process
Objective finding	Identifying problems and opportunities
Fact finding	Defining goals
Problem finding	Exploring possible strategies
Idea finding	Anticipating outcomes and act
Solution finding	Look back and learn
Acceptance finding	

Figure 1.4 The creative problem-solving process and the IDEAL problem-solving process.

☐ How to make more effective use of a manager's time

☐ How to improve a product's appeal to customers

☐ How to improve motivation among staff

☐ How to appeal to customer's wants and needs

☐ How to cut costs through more efficient/effective production methods

☐ How to identify new and profitable product-market opportunities

☐ How to get skilled and experienced staff to stay with the company without paying them excessively high salaries

Figure 1.5 Suitable management problems for creative problem solving.

production methods, to find new ways to motivate people, and so on. Creativity turns up in every business situation where there is a chance that things can be done in a more business-like, more profitable or in a more satisfying way. The list in Figure 1.5 shows typical management problems requiring creative thinking.

Problems which require creative thinking are 'open-ended' problems; that is, problems for which there is not just one solution.

Blocks to creative thinking

Despite the need for creative thinking there are many barriers to this in business. These include: a lack of resources and support from management to try out new ideas; functional 'myopic' thinking (seeing things only from the perspective of production, marketing, personnel or finance, for example); fear of criticism; resistance to change; fear of taking risks and incurring failure (one's job or career might be at stake); difficulty in seeing remote relationships; tendency to conform; an overemphasis on competition or cooperation (following up new ideas might be counter-productive);

negative attitudes towards creativity techniques; and blinkered thinking ('only one right way to do things' attitude).

A structured approach to creative thinking is therefore advocated to help, at least in part, overcome some of the barriers.

A structured approach to creative thinking

In creative thinking one has to put to one side beliefs that are held and sometimes entertain the impossible. Through a series of steps one may proceed to move from the impossible to the possible. Creative thinking and creative problem solving can be particularly difficult mental exercises. It would be extremely useful if there were some techniques which would help to circumvent these problems. Fortunately, much attention has indeed been given to this very subject. There are techniques which assist in problem identification, problem definition, idea generation, idea evaluation and idea implementation.

The use of creative problem-solving techniques may help to reduce many of the barriers to creativity in individuals and teams. These techniques can be intriguing and stimulating to use. The light-hearted nature which often accompanies the use of idea-generating aids, in particular, in a group setting encourages an environmentally friendly atmosphere and can lead to unusual patterns of thought.

The techniques will be discussed in detail in later chapters of this book but in this chapter we will briefly introduce them.

Problem identification and definition

Identifying problems is viewed as a very important activity and definition and redefinition of a problem rely on how objectives have been specified. There are specific techniques designed especially for the purpose of identifying, defining and redefining problems. Whichever is involved, the basic aim is to discover a new perspective on a focal problem. The reason for this is twofold. In the first instance the problem as given may have been incorrectly defined and this situation is therefore remedied through redefinitional procedures. Secondly, finding a new perspective on a problem should result in a different set of ideas being subsequently generated. Such alternative sets of ideas may be more useful than those generated without obtaining a new perspective on the problem.

There are two types of specific methods: *redefinitional techniques* and *analytical techniques*.

Redefinitional techniques include such methods as 'boundary examination', suggested by Edward De Bono (1970), 'goal orientation', put forward by Tudor Rickards (1974), the 'six honest serving men' approach as found in the Osborn–Parnes creative problem-solving model (see Parnes, Noller and Biondi, 1977) and 'progressive abstractions' as suggested by Geschka, Schaude and Schlicksupp (1973).

Analytical techniques include such methods as 'decomposable matrices', emanating from the work of Herbert Simon (1969), 'dimensional analysis', developed by Jensen (1978), 'input–output', developed at the General Electric Company, 'organised random search', suggested by Williams (1960) and 'relevance systems', outlined by Rickards (1974).

All the above methods are capable of producing new problem viewpoints and factoring a problem into its essential elements. They are discussed, along with other methods, in Chapter 4.

Idea generation methods

There are many different idea-generating methods. In fact, many techniques can be combined so that the potential number of methods is very large indeed. Four major techniques seem to dominate, however, and in this book attention is focused on these four major techniques along with techniques that have something in common with the four major ones. The four techniques are shown in Figure 1.6 and discussed briefly below.

Brainstorming

One of the most popular forms of brainstorming takes the form of a group activity; a group leader records all the ideas generated during the session on a flip-chart. Group members are invited to call out ideas relating to the problem as they occur. The aim is to generate as many ideas as possible – the wilder the ideas the better. Ideas are never evaluated during the generation process. By being able to see other people's ideas recorded, individuals are able to find new combinations or 'hitchhike or freewheel' on those ideas to produce new insights.

Synectics

Gordon (1961), credited with originating the techniques, emphasized the need to 'make the familiar strange' in order to increase the possibility of gaining new insights into problems. Synectics is a process for a group of individuals working on a problem in an unusual manner. The approach

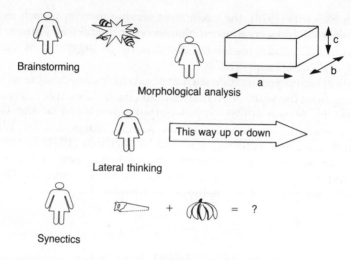

Figure 1.6 Four major creative problem-solving approaches.

emphasizes the non-rational substance of thought in the expectation that such a method will give an original, and certainly stimulating, slant to a problem. The use of metaphors encourages use of material which on first sight may seem altogether inapplicable to a problem.

As with brainstorming, the group leader is a facilitator–recorder of data and does not play any other active role in the proceedings. The other members of the group may number from five to ten and comprise people who may or may not have competent expertise in the subject matter to be considered.

Lateral thinking

De Bono (1970, 1971) envisages lateral thinking as a description of a mental process leading to new insights. For him, 'the twin aspects of lateral thinking are first the provocative use of information and second the challenge to accepted concepts'.

There are a number of operational techniques.

Morphological analysis

The creation of this technique is attributed to Zwicky (1969). The basic approach is, first, to list the possible dimensions that together describe a problem or system being studied. For example, if one was trying to identify possible new product ideas then one might consider such things as shape of the product, material from which it is made and potential end-use as three such dimensions.

The next step involves generating or listing attributes under the various dimensions that have been identified. Once the listing of attributes has been exhausted one then has to examine as many combinations of attributes across the identified dimensions as possible and pick out any promising or unusual ideas. The promising ideas may be evaluated subsequently for their suitability.

The above idea generation methods are explored in more detail in Chapters 5 to 8 inclusive, with related methods. In addition, Chapter 9 examines a number of other popular idea-generating techniques (for example, mind-mapping, force field analysis, etc.).

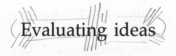

Evaluating ideas

Sometimes ideas which are generated can be evaluated fairly easily. Some may stand out as much more suitable solutions to identified problems than others. On other occasions we may want to try out several possible ideas and the ranking of the ideas is not particularly important. On other occasions, however, we may generate several or even many ideas and considerable uncertainty may exist with respect to which idea is to be preferred over another. In a situation where we have scarce resources and where it is desirable to implement a small proportion or even only one of the ideas we have generated then some method of ranking the ideas is desirable.

The simplest method of evaluating ideas involves constructing tables which allow us to compare the advantages and disadvantages of the various ideas (see Chapter 10). More sophisticated screening methods have been suggested by Hamilton (1974). These methods involve 'culling' ideas which fail to satisfy key criteria and rating and scoring ideas against desirable criteria. Many decisions are taken in a group situation and techniques which are specifically designed to take account of this include the 'Castle technique', suggested by O'Rourke (1984). Other useful evaluation methods include 'creative evaluation', suggested by Moore (1962), 'decision balance sheet', developed by Janis and Mann (1977), 'disjointed incrementalism', attributable to Braybrooke and Lindblom (1963), 'reverse brainstorming', described by Whiting (1958), and 'weighting systems'. These and other methods are considered in detail in Chapter 10.

Implementing ideas

Defining problems, generating insights and evaluating ideas are only part of the task of problem solving. Putting ideas into practice can be difficult, especially when there are obstacles to prevent their introduction and surmounting these obstacles represents the final stage in the problem-solving process. In fact, one of the factors which should be taken into account when evaluating ideas is the ease with which an idea can be implemented.

Blocks to implementation comprise such things as lack of adequate resources to implement ideas, lack of commitment and motivation in those required to implement ideas, resistance to change, procedural obstacles, perceived risk associated with implementing ideas, political undercurrents, lack of cooperation in the organization or a feeling of distrust, and so on.

A variety of tools or techniques can be used profitably to help to introduce new ideas in a systematic and planned way into an organizational setting. 'Consensus mapping', suggested by Hart and others (1985), helps participants to visualize, analyze and organize ideas that are sequence dependent. A graphic map is created which indicates ideas and shows how ideas are thought to be interdependent. Another useful method suggested by Kepner and Tregoe (1976) is 'potential problem analysis'. This method emphasizes a systematic approach for anticipating problems that are likely to prevent a project from being implemented. PERT networks and research planning diagrams are also useful tools for helping to implement newly generated ideas that involve a substantial time scale for implementation.

In addition to the systematic planning and introduction of ideas there is the task of persuading people who are going to make use of the ideas that they are worth using. Ideas may have to be sold to people who can authorize their implementation. This may ease the task of gaining subsequent motivation to ensure that new ideas are successful after they have been adopted. The task of implementing ideas is explored in Chapter 11.

Computer assisted creativity aids

General applications software can be used to assist creative problem solving at any of the various stages in the process. An electronic mail system facilitates the informal exchange of ideas. Spreadsheets allow the user to construct simple or complex mathematical models which make it easy to try out ideas which involve calculations – for example, sensitivity analyses. The manipulation and searching of databases can help solve customers' problems; external databases can be searched for information; marketing databases can supply the means to identify target customers. Planning or PERT software can assist in planning the implementation of ideas or solutions to problems.

In addition to general applications software of the kind discussed above, more specialized software is available for individuals who are involved in design and modelling. The use of such software speeds up the design and modelling processes involved.

There are also applications of information technology that have been expressly designed to assist in the generation of solutions to open-ended problems. At the simplest level they comprise programs that assist with the capture and restructuring of unstructured thoughts. More complex software has been developed that simulates well-known and tried creative problem-solving aids such as brainstorming and morphological analysis.

Group aids to creative thinking have also been emulated by computer decision support mechanisms. In addition to facilities for individuals, networked personal computers provide the surroundings for software able to assemble and amalgamate the ideas of different individuals. A team can use an application to evaluate and rank ideas which have either been generated in a group brainstorming session or which are the result of individual efforts collated on the network. This kind of software saves time and permits equality of opportunity to input ideas. It also facilitates the gaining of a consensus of opinion. Chapter 12 reviews recent developments in computer aided creative problem-solving.

References

Ackoff, R. L. and Vegara, E. (1988) 'Creativity in problem solving and planning', in R. L. Kuhn (ed.), *Handbook for Creative and Innovative Managers*, New York: McGraw Hill, 77–89.

Bennis, W. and Nanus, B. (1985) *Leaders: The strategies for taking charge*, New York: Harper & Row.

Bransford, J. D. and Stein, B. S. (1993) *The Ideal Problem Solver*, 2nd edn, New York: W. H. Freeman.

Braybrooke, D. and Lindblom, C. E. (1963) *A Strategy of Decision*, New York: The Free Press.

De Bono, E. (1970) *Lateral Thinking: Creativity step by step*, New York: Harper & Row.

De Bono, E. (1970, 1971) *Lateral Thinking for Management*, Cew York: McGraw-Hill (republished in Pelican).

Ekvall, G. and Parnes, S. (1988) 'Creative problem solving methods in product development', *Creativity and Innovation Yearbook*, 1, Manchester: Manchester Business School.

Geschka, H., Schaude, G. R. and Schlicksupp, H. (1973), 'Modern techniques for problem solving', *Chemical Engineering*, August, 91–7.

Gordon, W. J. (1961) *Synectics*, New York: Harper & Row.

Guilford, J. P. (1967) *The Nature of Human Intelligence*, New York: McGraw Hill.

Halpern, D. (1989) *Thought and Knowledge: An Introduction to Critical Thinking*, Hillsdale, NJ: Lawrence Erlbaum.

Hamilton, H. R. (1974) 'Screening business development opportunities', *Business Horizons*, August, 13–24.

Hart, S., Borousch, M., Enk, G. and Hornick, W. (1985) 'Managing complexity through consensus mapping: technology for the structuring of group decisions', *Academy of Management Review*, 10(3), 587–600.

Hayes, J. R. (1989) *The Complete Problem Solver*, 2nd edn, Hillsdale, NJ: Lawrence Erlbaum.

Isaksen, S. G. and Treffinger, D. J. (1985) *Creative Problem Solving: The Basic Course*, Buffalo, NY: Bearly.

Janis, I. L. and Mann, L. (1977) *Decision Making*, New York: The Free Press.

Jensen, J. V. (1978) 'A heuristic analysis of the nature and extent of a problem', *Journal of Creative Behaviour*, 12, 168–80.

Kelly, G. A. (1955) *The Psychology of Personal Constructs*, New York: Norton.

Kepner, C. H. and Tregoe, B. B. (1976) *The Rational Manager*, Princeton, NJ: Kepner-Tregoe.

Moore, L. B. (1962) 'Creative action – the evaluation, development and use of ideas', in S. J. Parnes and H. F. Harding (eds), *A Sourcebook for Creative Thinking*, New York: Scribner.

Newell, A. and Simon, H. A. (1972) *Human Problem Solving*, Englewood Cliffs, NJ: Prentice Hall.

O'Rourke, P. J. (1984) *The Castle Technique: How to achieve group consensus in a very short time with no argument*, Lyons, CO: Steamboat Valley Press.

Osborn, A. (1957) *Applied Imagination*, New York: Scribner.

Parnes, S. J., Noller, R. and Biondi, A. (1977) *Guide to Creative Action*, New York: Scribner.

Polya, G. (1957) *How To Solve It*, Garden City, New York: Doubleday Anchor.

Raudsepp, E. (1987) 'Establishing a creative climate', *Training and Development Journal*, April, 50–3.

Rickards, T. (1974) *Problem-Solving Through Creative Analysis*, Aldershot: Gower.

Rickards, T. (1988) 'Creativity and innovation: a transatlantic perspective', *Creativity and Innovation Yearbook*, Manchester: Manchester Business School.

Rogers, C. (1954) 'Towards a theory of creativity', *Review of General Semantics*, 11, 249–60.

Simon, H. A. (1969) *The Science of the Artificial*, Cambridge, Mass.: MIT Press.

Van Gundy, A. (1987) 'Organisational Creativity and Innovation', in S. G. Isaksen (ed.), *Frontiers of Creative Research: Beyond the basics*, pp. 358–79, Buffalo, NY: Bearly.

Van Gundy, A. B. (1988) *Techniques of Structured Problem Solving*, New York: Van Nostrand Reinhold.

Van Gundy, A. B. (1992) *Idea Power*, New York: American Management Association.

Wertheimer, M. (1945) *Productive Thinking*, New York: Harper & Row.

Whiting, C. S. (1958) *Creative Thinking*, New York: Van Nostrand Reinhold.

Williams, F. E. (1960) *Foundations of Creative Problem Solving*, Ann Arbor, MI: Edward Brothers.

Zwicky, F. (1969) *Discovery Invention Research Through the Morphological Approach*, New York: Macmillan.

2

Coping with blocks to creative problem solving

Creative insights often require people to see remote relationships. In going about our normal business this may be quite hard to do! For example, Velcro is a Swiss invention dating from 1948. Returning from a day hunting, the engineer Georges de Mestarl noticed that burdock seed heads clung to his clothing. Under the microscope he discovered that each of these heads was surrounded by minute hooks allowing them to catch onto fabrics. It then occurred to him to fix similar hooks on fabric strips which would cling together and serve as fasteners. Eight years were needed to develop the basic product: two nylon strips, one of which contained thousands of small hooks, and the other even smaller loops. When the two strips were pressed together they formed a quick and practical fastener. The invention was named Velcro from the French velours (velvet) and crochet (hook). But the interesting question is how many people would have seen the remote association in the first place?

People encounter uncertainty when trying to solve problems and make decisions. Almost inevitably, solutions are adopted or decisions taken which are afterwards considered to be less than satisfactory or even inappropriate. The implementation of such courses of action often results in unanticipated consequences and usually, faced with such eventualities, attempts are made to rectify the situation if this is possible. Rectifying errors arising in this way can be costly.

Inappropriate action often stems from an inability to think creatively. This inability is brought about by an invisible barrier, of which people are usually unaware.

To provide a framework for exploring how the blocks to creativity arise we will use the model of information processing and problem solving proposed by Newell and Simon (1972). We will recall from Chapter 1 that ideas from this model contributed to the IDEAL problem-solving model of Bransford and Stein (1993).

Information processing and problem solving

Problem solving involves processing information. Conceptualizing problem solving in this way, Newell and Simon (1972) (see Figure 2.1) argued that:

1. A person perceives raw data and processes these perceptions sufficiently to recognize the *task environment* – the components of the problem or the terms in which it is presented – that is the task as described by the person. For example, one might see falling profits in the balance sheet and see the task as one of explaining why profits are falling.

2. The information is next transformed into what might be described as a person's problem space – in other words, simply the way in which the person views the task. In this representation a person has to be quite clear about the goal – what has to be done; where he or she is in relationship to the *goal*, and what kinds of acts must be carried out to reach the goal. With respect to the profitability problem, introduced above, the goal is to explain the trend in profits. The individual knows that he or she cannot tell at a glance what is creating the falling profits, but from experience with similar problems will know that a known, systematic set of auditing procedures have to be followed to find a solution.

3. Depending upon how the problem space has been conceived, a person uses various kinds of information drawn from memory, or information that is given with the problem, to process data so as to move toward the goal. In the profitability example above, the person will have previous experience of examining accounts and will be able to make use of this information in the analysis. In addition, information is provided in the accounting data and by following auditing conventions the person will be able to make use of this data.

The total set of operations used in the effort to move from the initial perception of the data to the goal is what Newell and Simon call the production system or programme. In the course of carrying out the programme, a person will notice whether any step or series of steps reduces the distance to the goal. If this is the case then the person will continue with it but if not, he or she will move on to the next step or steps

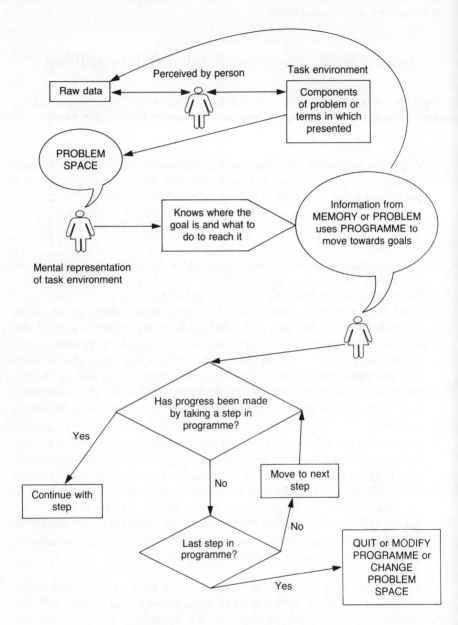

Figure 2.1 Newell and Simon model.

in the programme. If the entire programme fails to materialize in the attainment of the goal, then the person either quits, modifies the programme, or changes the problem space.

The conclusion that might be drawn from the analysis put forward by Newell and Simon is that problem solving involves the search for the most successful programme. However, as Minsky (1974) argues, problem solving may be not so much a search for a successful programme as a search for the best problem space. Whatever the case, it would seem logical that a good programme without a good problem space would be likely to be unproductive in terms of solution finding. Similar results will ensue in the case where there is a poor programme and a poor problem space. Problem space and programme, along with accurate perception of the task environment, are important components of the problem-solving process.

How blocks to problem solving can be explained in terms of the Newell and Simon model

Blocks to solution finding can arise because:

1. The task environment is perceived incorrectly – this can lead to mind-set (see below).
2. The problem space is incorrect – creative problem-solving techniques can help to structure problems, see later chapters in the book.
3. There is a lack of information, either with the problem or in memory. The solution is to generate more information either through information gathering (research), expert advice or even through stimulating thought patterns which would not normally be stimulated (see creative problem-solving methods later in the book).

In the following section we will look at how barriers to problem solving can be created by mind-set.

Mind-set

Mind-set is a condition where an individual is over-sensitized to some part of the information available at the expense of other parts (see Figure 2.2). It is often useful for people to have mind-sets. For example:

☐ It helps to become sensitized to some important things and serves us well – for example, red lights act as warnings and alert us to impending danger.

MIND-SET

Experience: we learn to solve problems by doing them

Where X is the problem,
        Y is the action and
        Z is the solution

When X occurs we do Y and the problem Z is solved

$$X \rightarrow Y \Rightarrow Z$$

This leads to doing Y every time X occurs and as long as Z occurs there is POSITIVE MIND-SET

However, if X occurs and we do Y but no solution, Z, is produced:

$$X \rightarrow Y \text{ NOT } Z$$

then this leads to NEGATIVE MIND-SET and it is difficult to unlearn something which has proved useful in the past

Figure 2.2   Positive and negative mind-set.

□ As a result of learning from experience, it sensitizes us to patterns that remind us of patterns which have enabled us to solve problems in the past. We do not have to re-invent the wheel each time we encounter the same kind of problem. If, when driving a car, we have experienced a skid and successfully dealt with the situation then when we subsequently encounter another skid situation we can deal with it using our acquired knowledge.

When mind-set blocks us: the Einstellung effect and functional fixedness

Luchins (1942) showed how mind-set, under certain conditions, may produce fixation and stereotyping in problem-solving behaviour. The condition may show itself under conditions where the individual has discovered a strategy that initially functions well in solving certain tasks, but later blocks the realization of new and simpler solutions to similar problems. The effect reflects a dysfunctional consequence of the normal rational way of approaching problems that may block the establishment of a new perspective and more important lines of procedure in task environments that resemble those encountered before. Cyert and March (1963) observed similar behaviour among practising managers in real-life contexts. Typical managerial search is seen as simple minded, and as over-emphasizing previous experience, by selectively searching in regions close to where previous solutions have been found.

Duncker (1945) investigated how past experience may block productive problem solving. He coined the phrase 'functional fixedness' to refer to a block against using an object in a new way that is required to solve a problem. Some interesting examples of how the factor of functional fixedness may operate in real-life contexts and seriously hamper the process of technical invention are given by Weizenbaum (1984). According to the latter the steam engine had been in use for a hundred years to pump water out of mines before Trevithick had the idea of using it as a source of locomotive power; it was seen *only* as a tool to help pump water out of mines. Another example is the computer, that for a long time was seen simply as a calculator before its potential as a general symbol manipulator was conceived.

Clearly, while mind-set can provide us with substantial benefits unfortunately there are times when it does not serve us well. In addition to the examples above, early work on aircraft pilot error showed how pilots expected the dials to be showing their normal readings and failed to notice when they showed abnormal readings. The solution to this kind of problem, of course, suggests that one should not rely on the visual sight of the pilot alone when monitoring events concerning the flight of an aircraft.

In the same way mind-set can also create difficulties for executives when they are faced with new or novel problems. Since the problem is a new one that they have never encountered before, it is likely that executives will find difficulty in solving such a problem. When stuck on a problem managers tend to follow their mind-set, which may not be able to help when a new kind of problem situation is encountered for the first time. For example, marketing executives know how to react to probable competitive strategies of firms which have been competing within their industry for some time. New entrants to the industry, however, are an unknown entity and may be much more difficult to compete against.

Mind-set is often characterized by 'one right answer' thinking, negative or 'yes but' thinking, or over-regard for logical thinking.

The fact that executives have solved a problem in a particular way in the past and always achieved 100 per cent success reinforces their belief in themselves. If it has worked before then there would not seem to be any reason why it should not work again. This can lead to a situation where it is believed that there is only one right answer. When this fails to provide a solution to a new problem executives become stuck and do not know what to do.

Negative or 'yes but' thinking is commonly encountered in business. Executives are naturally keen to ensure that a project will stand a good chance of being a success. Every suggestion is therefore questioned or criticized to make sure that an optimal decision is taken. Unfortunately, the process of criticism itself can stifle creative thinking (see below). It is better to use the phrase 'yes and' rather than 'yes but'. For example, faced with the suggestion of making redundancies, the normal response might be:

'yes, but that will only lead to unrest on the shop floor and possible strike action.'

The better response would be:

'yes and wouldn't it be useful, since we can then employ those people who are redundant in other jobs in the company.'

An over-regard for logical thinking can also create a barrier to creative thinking. Faith itself is not based on pure logical reasoning and we have to accept that many things happen in life which we may have some difficulty in explaining away in a logical fashion. This is not to say that creative thinking is illogical or requires the abandonment of logical reasoning. However, some of the methods we use to stimulate creative thinking certainly take us away from logical reasoning. Perhaps the main danger in an over-reliance on logical reasoning is that when logic fails there does not seem to be any solution to a problem, if one depends upon logical reasoning alone.

Other barriers to creative problem solving

Many researchers have attempted to address the phenomenon of barriers to creativity. These include Arnold, 1962; Adams, 1974; Jones, 1987; and Majaro, 1988 and they have all produced detailed lists of the various kinds of barriers to creative problem solving.

On one hand there are thought to be barriers limiting an individual's creative output that are related to the people themselves. On the other hand there are thought to be those that emanate from the environment in which the person exists (the focus of Majaro's interest). Personal barriers may be subdivided into physiological barriers, such as the perceptual limitations of the senses or the brain's data-handling capacity, and psychological barriers related to the person's behaviour or attitudes.

Barriers for individuals

Arnold (1962) suggested:

1. Perceptual blocks, which prevent a person receiving a true, relevant picture of the outside world.

☐ Strategic blocks: 'one right answer approaches', inflexibility in thinking

☐ Value blocks: 'over-generalized ridigity influenced by personal values'

☐ Perceptual blocks: 'over-narrow focus of attention and interest'

☐ Self-image blocks: poor effectiveness through fear of failure, timidity in expressing ideas, etc.

Figure 2.3 Four typologies of blocks, according to Jones.

2. Cultural blocks, which result from influences of society.

3. Emotional blocks such as fear, anxiety and jealousy.

Adams (1974) effectively added a fourth category to those suggested by Arnold:

4. Intellectual and expressive blocks.

Jones (1987) identified four typologies of blocks. The typologies are shown in Figure 2.3 and discussed below.

Strategic blocks
Strategic blocks are exemplified by such things as 'vertical thinking', 'one right answer thinking' and 'either/or' thinking. They have the effect of causing problem solvers to think in ways which exclude consideration of all possible solutions. This can result in the implementation of an inappropriate solution (*mind-set*).

Value blocks
Value blocks reflect a person's beliefs. Strongly held beliefs can have the effect of making it impossible for a person to consider certain solutions to a problem.

Perceptual blocks
Perceptual blocks reflect the fact that executives may be overlooking opportunities or failing to anticipate threats as early as might otherwise be possible. Someone with a reputation for being a poor listener may suffer from this problem.

Self-image blocks
Self-image blocks reflect the fact that the individual is insufficiently robust to resist social pressures that reject any new idea at the outset.

Jones's approach has resulted in training applications which centre on

Lack of resources and support from management to
try out new ideas

Bureaucracy and red tape

Functional myopic thinking

Fear of criticism

Resistance to change

Fear of taking risks

Tendency to conform

Emphasis on management control

Rigid hierarchical structures

Tendency to look for one big winner

Figure 2.4 Organizational blocks to creativity.

personal feedback and counselling, including suggestions of the most appropriate mechanisms for developing improved skills. Strategic blocks can be challenged through creative problem solving training. Values, however, are a more difficult problem – but creating an awareness of personal values in the individual offers some respite. Perceptual blocks can be freed through observation and self-image blocks can profit from assertiveness training.

The argument is that the four blocks to problem solving impinge on how people perceive the task environment, draw up their problem space and develop their 'programme' for finding a solution to a problem.

So far we have looked at individual blocks to creative problem solving. Many problems are to be found where a group of individuals work together. In the next section we will look at the problems of organizational blocks.

Blocks in an organizational setting

Majaro (1988) linked barriers to creativity to organizational factors. He suggested that, while some of these could be removed, others are an integral part of the firm's history and tradition and can only be circumvented.

In fact, there are many barriers to creative thinking in organizations. These are shown in Figure 2.4 and discussed below.

Lack of resources and management support

A lack of resources and support from management to try out new ideas shows the absence of any organizational slack.

Creativity does require a certain amount of slack in an organization and the absence thereof can act as a barrier to the successful implementation of the whole process. This can present management with a real problem: if one wants to run a 'tight ship' with no floating spare manpower, one is running the risk of weakening the firm's ability to innovate. Spare manpower or under-utilized resources are an anathema to modern management.

Nevertheless, firms that have a certain level of slack are in a far better position to generate ideas and identify valuable commercial innovations. Moreover, they are the kind of firms that are well placed, if the need arises, to field a task force to manage and implement a rush of innovative ideas. Companies that have deliberately reduced the available slack in their system can be extremely productive in terms of output per capita, but will find that their creative output is fairly limited.

Bureaucracy and red tape

Bureaucracy can be the blight of creativity. It can reduce the ability of companies to innovate. Bureaucracy is the opposite of flexibility and the latter is an integral part of being creative. Bureaucracy can act as a barrier to the development of a more creative organization. If management really wants to improve the creativity and innovation of the organization it must, at the same time, take steps to reduce the negative effects of the bureaucratic machine.

Functional 'myopic' thinking

Functional myopic thinking could be defined as seeing things only from the perspective of production, marketing, personnel or finance, for example.

Many enterprises are organized along functional lines, as by and large this speeds up the efficiency with which work can be carried out. Unfortunately, one of the side effects of this kind of organizational structure is that it leads to functional units developing their own identities, reflecting a particular point of view of the organization as a whole. Marketers may believe, for instance, that successful innovation must start with the customer. It may be argued that unless one sets off by trying to establish what the customer really wants then there is little likelihood of achieving the customer satisfaction that is integral to the success of an innovation. While this is based upon sound logic if it is carried to its extreme, internally developed creativity and innovation may well be stifled.

Fear of criticism

It is a basic human shortcoming that people do not like to be criticized for their actions or ridiculed for their ideas. People are least likely to put forward their ideas when they fear that this going to happen.

Resistance to change

Creativity and innovation are associated with change. This may mean change in working habits or organization, reassignment of work or responsibilities, change in working methods, introduction of entirely new products or processes for manufacture and marketing, and so on.

Fear of taking risks and incurring failure (one's job or career might be at stake)

New products and projects involve risk. The risk may be financial in so far as the company's profitability is concerned. Alternatively, it may be associated with product liability to customers in that it may involve introducing a comparatively unknown product or service which has only had limited tests with users.

High risk projects can have catastrophic consequences should anything go wrong and can lead to a situation of entrapment for those involved in the venture. Entrapment occurs when people become over-committed to a project which is failing but experience difficulty in withdrawing from the project (Proctor, 1993).

Tendency to conform

Non-conformity with group norms is often considered to be eccentric behaviour. There is a danger if people are thought to be eccentric then their opinions and ideas will not be taken seriously by other members of the group. This puts pressure on people not to be too outlandish in their thinking and to go along with the general view of the group.

Emphasis on managerial control

Traditional financial controls are not appropriate for long-term innovation efforts. Very often financial control reflects short-range thinking where the focus is on quick returns with financially measurable results. Innovation and creativity may be much longer term and may not be readily measurable in terms of financial return.

Ideas are often overanalysed

Wanting to be too sure or too certain that something is a good idea can often result in loss of time and competitive advantage while efforts are expended to check out the idea. With the loss of time may come the loss of surprise and impact, not to speak of the originality of the idea.

Rigid hierarchical structures

Creativity and innovation are perhaps most needed in an unpredictable environment. This in turn requires a responsive organizational structure that can respond quickly to the needs of the situation. Too often, creativity and innovation are crushed under the weight of the monolithic structure of the organization.

Tendency to look for one big potential winner, rather than a number of smaller ones

Football pools firms have operated successfully for years on the basis of serving the human syndrome of day-dreaming. This phenomenon also permeates into organizations: people dream of making the one major breakthrough which takes them far ahead of the competition. Much effort is often wasted looking for the major breakthrough and good small opportunities can often be overlooked.

A climate for creativity and innovation

Having looked at the various factors that are thought to stifle creativity and innovation we need to consider how we can develop a climate in which both creativity and innovation can flourish. We can examine how organizations can create a climate for creativity and innovation by looking at the people, the process and the structure.

People

Prudent risk-taking should be the norm
The first suggestion is that people should be encouraged to undertake some risk in their work. To do this one must, of course, define limits clearly with respect to what losses can be sustained without punitive action being taken against the person concerned (see Figure 2.5).

Creating and maintaining an innovative climate begins at the top
The fostering of a creative and innovative climate within an organization is best originated from the higher echelons of the organization. This is particularly important when trying to create some degree of autonomy and prudent risk-taking behaviour within the organization.

Management should respond positively to new ideas
New ideas often spell out change and managers with established procedures and practices that seem to be operating effectively may well resist anything that threatens to change the status quo. Management should be encouraged to respond positively to new ideas, as long as there are sound benefits to be gained by so doing.

Generating creative ideas requires freedom of thought – some degree of autonomy
Removal of supervision and the giving of greater autonomy in decision making can lead to innovative and creative actions.

Linking specific performance to rewards
Motivation, to be creative and innovative, is linked with matching rewards to performance.

Prudent risk-taking

Creating and maintaining an innovative climate begins at the top

Management should respond positively to new ideas

Generating creative ideas requires freedom of thought

Linking specific performance to rewards

Provision of adequate financial resources

Creating a spirit of teamwork

Exposure to outside ideas

Conducting problem-solving retreats

Figure 2.5   Climate for creativity and innovation: people.

Provision of adequate financial resources
Creativity and innovation cannot be achieved without adequate resourcing. This not only means some organizational slack but also that financial resources have to be made available to get projects off the ground.

Creating a spirit of teamwork
There have to be opportunities for informal social interaction to ensure full understanding of organizational goals. A good ploy is to look for ways to create light-hearted competition among work groups.

Exposure of employees to outside ideas
Not only is it a good idea to get the different viewpoint of organizational members but it can also be beneficial to make use of outside speakers and in-house newsletters.

Conduct problem-solving retreats
Problems can be difficult to deal with in the work situation. Often, when we move away from the environment in which we encounter the problem to one which is entirely different and even new, solutions may be more easily found.

Process

A continual flow of ideas is required
Ideas do not always arise when they are needed most. That is why it is good strategy to have a system continually generating ideas (see Figure 2.6). Some of the ideas may very well end up looking for problems! But then, when the problem arises, the solution can be found immediately.

Review or revise suggestion schemes
It is important to make clear the process for evaluating ideas and dispensing rewards.

Establish an innovation council
Creativity and innovation need to be recognized as important activities within the organization. Recognition can be made through the formation of a council specifically set up to look at new ideas and initiatives.

Provide time for 'pet' projects
Not all the best and most profitable ideas arise as the result of formal problem-orientated thinking or research. Ideas often arise as a result of people being allowed to follow their own initiatives and 'pet' projects. Of

A continual flow of ideas is required
Review or revise suggestion schemes
Establish an innovation council
Provide time for 'pet' projects

Figure 2.6   Climate for creativity and innovation: process.

course, people can be allowed to spend an inordinate amount of time on such ventures but a modicum of discretion in this respect can pay substantial dividends.

Structure

Differentiate the structure
An organization must have specialized functions to respond to constantly changing forces in its external environment. In the case of a small firm this means that it is necessary to have people with a specialist orientation who can deal with specific functional aspects of the business. For example, the chief executive usually takes on marketing responsibilities when a firm is very small, but as the firm grows the job can be given to a specialist marketing manager or director. Similarly, specialist roles can develop in manufacturing, research and development (R&D) and personnel (see Figure 2.7).

Different viewpoints should not only be tolerated but should actually be encouraged
Creativity arises when a problem is viewed from different perspectives so that new insights can be obtained. This means that within an organization it is important to have different views and opinions aired on what are key or vitally important matters. Within the formal structure of the organization this can be achieved by using liaison positions, cross-departmental task forces and special integrating departments.

Establish creativity rooms containing books and idea-generating aids
In this book I argue the case for structured aids to creative problem solving. Structured problem-solving aids and methods can help to generate ideas and should be seen as part and parcel of the process of management creativity.

Improve the R&D–marketing interface – spell out how the two should interact
Ideas can arise both in R&D and in the course of the marketing personnel's

Differentiate the structure

Encourage different viewpoints

Establish creativity rooms containing idea-generating aids

Improve the R&D–marketing interface

Introduce cross-training – train people in different functional areas

Figure 2.7   Climate for creativity and innovation: structure.

interaction with the user of the product or service. To rely upon one of these sources to the exclusion of the other is extremely bad practice. People may want or need certain products or services; R&D can engineer appropriate designs to meet the requirements of customers, provided that they understand the exact nature of the customer requirements. Similarly, R&D may come up with excellent ideas but these ideas need to be tried out with users before any commitment is made to develop the products or services in a commercial way. Users can suggest potential improvements even to the best of ideas generated by R&D.

Introduce cross-training – train people in different functional areas
The more people know and understand about all aspects of the business the more likely it is that they will be able to come up with useful insights into difficult problems.

References

Adams, J. L. (1974) *Conceptual Blockbusting*, New York: W. H. Freeman.

Arnold, J. E. (1962) 'Education for innovation', in S. J. Parnes and H. F. Harding (eds), *A Sourcebook for Creative Thinking*, New York: Scribner.

Bransford, J. D. and Stein, B. S. (1993) *The Ideal Problem Solver*, New York: W. H. Freeman.

Cyert, R. N. and March, J. G. (1963) *A Behavioural Theory of the Firm*, Englewood Cliffs, NJ: Prentice Hall.

Duncker, K. (1945) 'On problem solving', *Psychological Monographs*, 58.

Jones, L. S. (1987) 'The development and testing of a psychological instrument to measure barriers to effective problem solving', unpublished Master's thesis, University of Manchester.

Luchins, A. A. (1942) 'Mechanization problem solving: the effect of Einstellung', *Psychological Monographs*, 54.

Majaro, S. (1988) *The Creative Gap*, London: Longman.

Minsky, M. (1974) 'A framework for representing knowledge', Cambridge, Mass.: MIT Artificial Intelligence Laboratory, Artificial Intelligence Memo No. 306.

Morgan, J. S. (1968) *Improving Your Creativity on the Job*, New York: American Management Association.

Newell, A. and Simon, H. A. (1972) *Human Problem Solving*, Englewood Cliffs, NJ: Prentice Hall.

Proctor, T. (1993) 'Entrapment in product development', *Creativity and Innovation Research Journal*, **2**(4), 260–5.

Weizenbaum, J. (1984) *Computer Power and Human Reason*, Harmondsworth: Penguin.

3

Theories of creativity

What is creative thinking?

The mathematician Poincaré expressed the thoughts of many distinguished scientists on the origin of ideas when he said:

When we arrived at Coutances, we got into a brake to go for a drive, and, just as I put my foot on the step, the idea came to me, though nothing in my former thoughts seemed to have prepared me for it . . . (Poincaré, 1952).

The same point was further developed by Mary Henle (1962):

Perhaps the most astonishing thing about creative thinking is that creative thinkers can tell us so little about it.

Creativity is a concept we often come across in our everyday life. One hears of creative people, admires creative objects of art or reads creative books. Yet despite our almost innate understanding of what it means to be creative there is much confusion about what creativity really is.

Creative thinking is an important feature of all aspects of organizational decision making. It is the phenomenon of awakening new thoughts, rearranging old learning and examining assumptions to formulate new theories and paradigms, or create awareness. It is the process of revealing, selecting, swapping around, and blending one's stock of facts, ideas and skills (see Figure 3.1).

Picasso captures the conceptual ideas of creativity quite succinctly in the following comments:

With me a picture is a sum of destruction. I make a picture and proceed to destroy it. But in the end, nothing is lost; the red I have removed

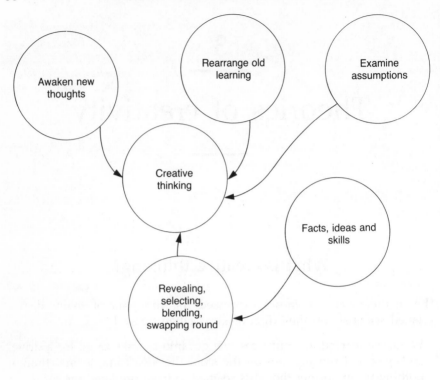

Figure 3.1 The nature of creativity.

from one part shows up in another. It would be very interesting to record photographically not the stages of a painting but its metamorphoses. One would see, perhaps, by what course a mind finds its way toward the crystallization of its dream. But what is very curious is to see that the picture does not change basically, the initial appearance remains almost intact in spite of appearances. I often see a light and a dark when I have put them in my picture. I do everything I can to 'break them up' by adding a colour that creates a counter effect . . . (Picasso's conversation with Christian Zervos, 1932)

This is Picasso the technician, who had a thorough understanding of his own craft. Picasso's comments were reflected later by the renowned psychologist Wertheimer (1945) when he described creativity as the breaking down and restructuring of thoughts about a topic in order to gain new insights into its nature. Rickards (1988), on the other hand, describes creativity as an 'escape from mental stuckness', an operational definition very much in keeping with its role in decision making and problem solving.

This chapter is concerned with how ideas arise and what can be done to assist people in obtaining insights into problems. Locke (1690) asserted that the source of all ideas is human experience and observation, an argument that will be pursued at some length here.

What are ideas?

One might think of ideas as 'the sentences of thought'. Ideas are mental phenomena which somehow drift into the mind, wander through it and often vanish into obscurity, never to be recalled again. Making notes on ideas as they arise is extremely important. Graham Wallas (1926) tells the story of a man 'who had so brilliant an idea that he went into his garden to thank God for it, but found on rising from his knees that he had forgotten it, and never recalled it'!

In terms of problem solving we might prefer to think of 'insights' rather than ideas. The gaining of insights into a problem can lead to a restructuring of that problem and the development of further insights into its solution. There may not be a perfect solution to a problem requiring creative thought but only different solutions, more acceptable solutions and, often, only further insights into a problem.

How do ideas arise?

Many ideas appear to arise purely by chance. Fleming discovered the effects of penicillin quite by accident – it was blown in from an open window and killed bacteria in a saucer containing a strain that he was investigating.

Laennec, in searching for a way to hear the sounds of the heart, found his answer when he noticed two boys using a see-saw in an unusual way. One was hitting one end of the wooden see-saw with a stone while the other listened with his ear pressed close to the other end of the see-saw. The idea of the stethoscope leapt to Laennec's mind.

Westinghouse discovered the idea of the air-brake when he casually read in a journal that compressed air power was being used by Swiss engineers in tunnel building.

Kekulé gained his clue to the nature of the benzene ring from his dream of a snake swallowing its own tail.

The BBC's 6.30 p.m. *Look North* TV news programme (21 April, 1993) reported that a nun from Leigh in Lancashire, when using her rosary beads, got the idea of using them to teach children to count and she subsequently set up a business. Children interviewed in the programme found the beads very useful and better than counting frames. As one little girl put it: 'When you drop them on the floor the beads stay where they are and you don't lose count of where you are up to.'

Generating ideas, however, is not simply a chance process. Ideas appear to arise by chance only when people are actually looking for ideas. It does not happen to people who are not curious or inquiring or who are not engaged in a search for opportunities, possibilities, answers or inventions.

It is also widely recognized that immersion in one's subject matter can be an important factor in gaining creative insights. Newton, for example, arrived at the law of gravitation by thinking about the problem for most of the time. It is also known that Einstein tried for years to clarify the problem of the relation of mechanical movement to electromagnetic phenomena. Creative insights appear to be easiest to gain in fields where we have considerable prior knowledge and experience and in relation to problems that we know a great deal about.

Motivation also plays an important role in our ability to be creative. Again there is a paradox, for creative work demands both a passionate interest on the part of the thinker and a certain degree of detachment from the work and ideas. Creative thinking, however, does not appear to occur where the individual's interest in the subject matter is relatively low. There seems to be a delicate balance whereby the creative thinker has to remain sufficiently detached from the work in order to examine it critically and if necessary reject or even destroy the work.

Theories of creativity

Two brain theory

Roger Sperry and his associates (Le Boeuf, 1990) at the California Institute of Technology, in their historic split-brain experiments, were able to separate surgically and test the thinking abilities of each half of the human brain. In so doing they found that each half of the brain has its own way of thinking and its own memories. The left brain tends to think in terms of symbols and words while the right brain thinks in terms of sensory images. The left brain is used for logical thinking, judgement, speaking and mathematical reasoning, while the right brain is the source of dreaming, feeling, visualization and intuition.

Creative thinking requires coordinating and using both sides of the brain (see Figure 3.2). Flashes of insight and intuition are the result of right brain thinking but analyzing these insights is the function of the left brain. Research into the thought processes of highly creative people shows

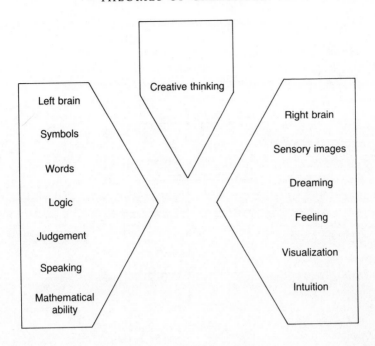

Figure 3.2 Creative thinking makes use of both halves of the brain.

that they rely heavily on the intuitive side of their brain. Einstein relied heavily on visual thinking before transforming his thoughts into precise equations.

The process of creative thinking

While the two brain theory suggests an anatomical approach to creativity it does little to explain the processes involved. Wallas (1926) distinguished four stages of thought: preparation, incubation, illumination and verification (Figure 3.3). Incubation, according to Wallas, was a period of inactivity or change of activity after the input of information, which seems to promote creative thought. According to Wallas, incubation covers two different phenomena. First, during incubation people do not consciously think about a particular problem. Secondly, a series of unconscious mental events may take place during this period. Although 'incubation' represents a favourable condition for creative insights, little was known of how it operated.

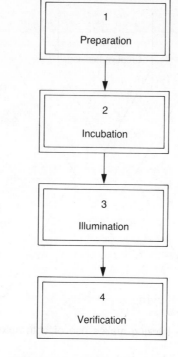

Figure 3.3   Wallas's four stages.

To understand the processes involved in the origin of creativity we have to turn to the schools of thought (Henry, 1991):

- Grace
- Accident
- Personality
- Association
- Cognitive

Grace

Creativity is really something of a mystery. Insights, imaginative efforts, illumination and intuition seem to come from nowhere. One might even look upon it as having magical qualities – something which is outside of normally being human. The phenomenon of genius exemplifies this notion, since creative artists, musicians and writers all seem to possess extraordinary potential. Creativity in this sense is seen as a divine gift.

Accident

This is the opposite of creativity being a divine gift: it simply arises by chance. Van Andel (1989) offers various types of accidental discoveries, such as those of immunization arising from an interruption in work, radioactivity from the wrong hypothesis and the smallpox vaccination from observation. There are also the examples given earlier in this chapter.

Personality

This point of view considers creativity to be a natural human trait and an intrinsic part of life. Human beings possess various attributes and capabilities to varying degrees. Many things can be learnt and perhaps the capacity for creative actions is not so much a personality trait as a state of mind which can be learnt. Some people seem to have a facility for creative thinking, while others do not. Nevertheless, with practice people can improve. We have seen in the previous chapter that there are mental barriers to thinking creatively, so by adopting this theoretical stance we might concentrate on removing mental barriers to creativity in people.

Association

This is the most popular theoretical perspective and it suggests that applying procedures from one area of knowledge to another can give rise to novel associations, and that such associations can form the basis of creative ideas. The notion was popularized by Koestler (1967) under the term bisociation, and it underlies the justification of many divergent thinking techniques.

Cognitive

Perkins (1981) and Weisburg (1986) argue that there is nothing peculiarly special about creativity and that it draws upon perfectly normal cognitive processes such as recognition, reasoning and understanding. The essence of this argument is the notion that chance favours a prepared mind. Perkins (1981) quotes Sternberg as arguing that insight depends on three processes: selective *encoding of information*, selective *combination* – that is, synthesizing appropriate information, and selective *comparison* – relating new information to old.

The cognitive view stresses the part played by application – the fact that many inventors work at a problem for years. Hayes (1989) concluded that

10 years of intense preparation were needed to produce outstanding creative contributions. The logic of the cognitive position is that deep thinking about an area over a long period leaves the discoverer informed enough to notice anomalies that might be significant. Perkins (1981) acknowledges that there is something different in the character of the mind that is attracted to particularly difficult and complex problems. Highly creative people are strongly motivated and seem able to concentrate over a long period.

The cognitive approach offers one of the best ways of understanding creative thinking and we will explore it in more depth below.

The cognitive theory of creativity

Cognitive processes have been a much disputed topic for many years. Various schools of psychology, the psychoanalytical, *Gestalt* and associative, all have their various perspectives on the subject.

At the core of the thinking process is memory. It is accepted that there is both long-term and short-term memory. Short-term memory can hold only a small amount of information at any one time. Long-term memory, on the other hand, has a vast information storage capacity. If we paid attention to all the things that our senses are reporting at any particular moment and took them all into consideration it would be very hard for us to decide what to do. We can only hold a few things in our short-term memory and that is what enables us to focus on what is important and to act quickly.

Long-term memory may be thought of as being filled with all the images, sounds, odours and other types of sensory data in an assembled form and which we hold as a symbolic picture of our remembered information. Information itself is learned from our experience and stored in chunks ('chunking') along with cues associated with the information (Figure 3.4).

We can often recall the wanted material by recalling the unwanted accompaniment. The learned material and the cues form complex networks of information. Thus when we are trying to think of objects that might resemble 'red faces' we may find it easier not to concentrate in our minds on 'faces' but rather to make connections with similar images – beetroots, the setting sun, etc. (Figure 3.5). From a creativity point of view it is how we make the connections along and across these networks that is of interest.

According to the connectionist, or parallel distributed processing model, proposed by McClelland (1981) information about people, events and

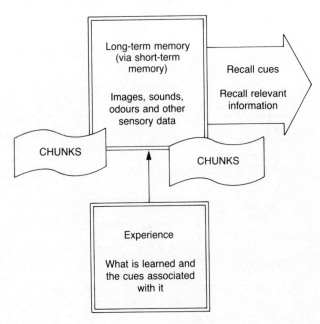

Figure 3.4 Storing information and retrieving chunks of information from memory.

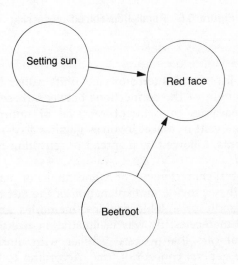

Figure 3.5 Similar images.

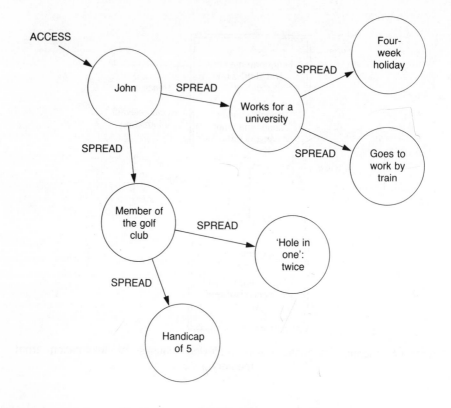

Figure 3.6 Parallel distributed processing.

objects is stored in several interconnected units rather than in a single location. The strength of the connections between these units increases as a result of learning. Subsequent retrieval of information about a particular person, event or object involves gaining access to one or more of the relevant units, followed by a spread of activation to other relevant units (Figure 3.6).

One of the general characteristics of connectionist or parallel distributed networks is that they provide an explanation of the fact that we seem to possess both episodic or autobiographical memories and semantic, or knowledge-based memories. By way of illustration, we possess information about several cars that we are familiar with, and we also have knowledge of the general concept of 'car'. According to McClelland and Rumelhart (1986), the stimulus word 'car' leads to activation of several units referring to specific cars, and an averaging process indicates the typical features of cars in general (Figure 3.7).

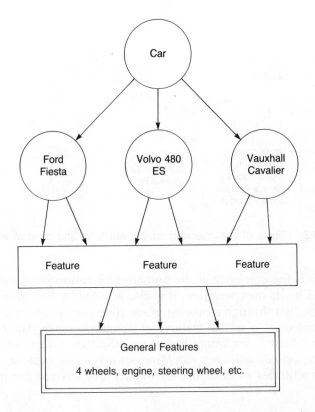

Figure 3.7 Activation of episodic and semantic memories.

The brain as a human information processing system

The process of thinking effectively means accessing very large volumes of information in long-term memory via a 'bottleneck' memory space, which takes the form of short-term memory (Figure 3.8). While the speed of access to long-term memory is extremely rapid it appears possible to consider only small amounts of information at a time. 'Bottlenecks' are symptomatic of inefficient operation and usually result in a slow down or cessation of operation if they become overloaded or choked. This view of the human information processing system points to limitations in terms of its efficiency. In problem solving or trying to think creatively we immediately come up against these limitations. Creative problem solving aids need to help us circumvent these difficulties if they are to be useful aids to thinking.

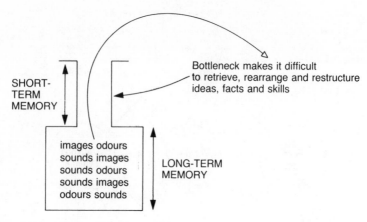

Figure 3.8 Effects of bottlenecking on our ability to find creative solutions.

Not only is the efficiency of the human information processing system constrained by its own structure, it is also affected by how people use it. It is thought that through a process of selective perception or filtering we pay attention only to certain features of things we sense. The concept of a perceptual filter is important because of the factors that constrain it – for instance, beliefs, attitudes, etc. Mind-set may occur because of various beliefs and attitudes we hold and the impact they have on our perceptual filter.

How knowledge is stored in memory

It is important to understand how knowledge is stored in human memory. This enables us to appreciate how long-term memory may be organized and how the search of long-term memory may be conducted. Among the earliest ideas on representation were those of Quillian (1968), who introduced the notion of the 'semantic network' (Figure 3.9). This maintained that knowledge can be represented by a kind of directed, labelled graph structure in which the basic structural element is a set of interrelated nodes.

In Figure 3.9 we see that a person perceives the office to be an unpleasant place associated with arguments and meetings. The meetings themselves are associated with problems arising from discontent over workloads. It will also be seen that there are various other interconnections. Semantic network theory has a place in the structure of representation, but it does not allow one to structure knowledge into higher-order representational units. Nevertheless, as we shall see later in the book, externalizing this

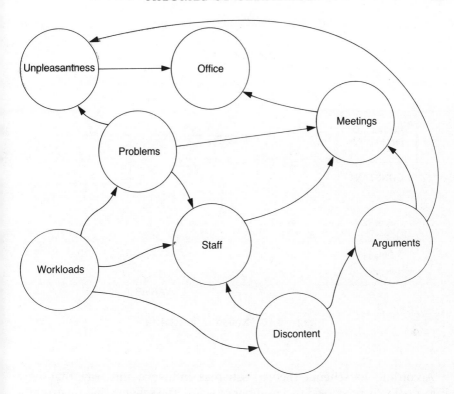

Figure 3.9 Part of a semantic network.

form of representation can be used effectively in facilitating creative thinking.

It is the major function of 'schemas' to add a structure which allows for the encoding of more complex interrelationships among lower level units (see Rumelhart and Norman, 1983). Schemas are learned as a result of experience and reside in memory to be called upon at any time. Schemas are packets of information in which there is a fixed part, representing those characteristics which are always true of exemplars of the concept and a variable part, which need not always be true. The schema for the concept of 'elephant' would contain constant parts such as 'an elephant has a trunk' and variable parts such as 'an elephant can be found in a zoo'. Variables have default values if the incoming information is unspecified. Thus the concept 'pensioner' might have as its fixed part 'is retired from his or her former occupation', but unless the variable 'age' is specified this would tend to default to 'old' (Figure 3.10). Schemas can also be embedded within one another so that a schema consists of a configuration of subschemas, and so on.

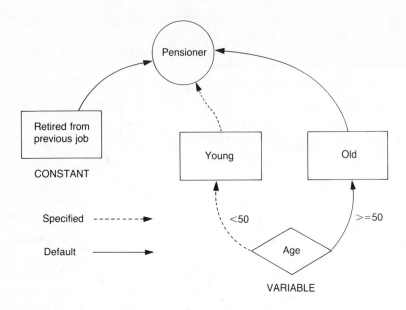

Figure 3.10   Notion of a schema.

According to schema theory, schemas influence the way that new information is processed in a number of ways. The schema that is currently activated guides the selection of what is encoded and stored in memory, so that information relevant to that schema is more likely to be remembered than non-relevant information. The schema provides a framework within which the information can be stored and which can be used at retrieval to guide search processes.

SCRIPTS, DELTACTS and MOPS

Workers in the area of Artificial Intelligence have made important contributions to cognitive science. This perspective suggests that we make use of specific types of schemas known as SCRIPTS and DELTACTS (Schank and Abelson, 1977) in dealing with problems. SCRIPTS allow people to make inferences about a situation and are put together from smaller data elements called MOPS (memory organization packets). MOPS serve to organize experiences around essential similarities, enabling people to recognize old situations in new guises and to draw conclusions.

SCRIPTS are stereotyped responses based on experience. It is argued that in trying to cope with a new situation or problem people try to recall previous ways in which they have dealt with similar problems: they try to recall a SCRIPT. A SCRIPT is an organized memory structure that describes a suitable sequence of activities to deal with a particular problem or situation.

SCRIPTS guide what people do, think and say. Retrieving an appropriate SCRIPT from memory allows people to deal with a situation or a problem in an effective manner.

Schank and Abelson (1977) suggested that people undertake 'goal directed behaviour' to cope with problems or situations where a relevant SCRIPT cannot be retrieved, because they have never learned one in the first instance. Discovering the goal may be part of the process and sometimes the goal may have to be implied from several aspects of a description. Furthermore, one has to establish a set of ways in which to satisfy the main goal. These take the form of subgoals and associated plans which Schank and Abelson termed 'DELTACTS'.

Schank and Abelson (1977) argued that higher-level structures, which they termed THEMES, serve as nuclei around which GOALS, PLANS and SCRIPTS are organized (Figure 3.11). In trying to solve a problem it is suggested that we organize our thoughts around a theme. For example, imagine that the boss has decided to remove the opportunity of earning extra money from people working in the department. There are various possible approaches that could be taken but one THEME that could emerge is that of challenging his or her authority to prevent people earning extra money. SCRIPTS, DELTACTS, etc. would be organized around the THEME of 'Challenge Authority' and as a consequence solutions to emerge might be such things as 'appeal to a higher authority in the organization' or, if it were possible, 'flout the boss's authority'.

How we get ideas: the 'index metaphor'

Building on the concept of SCHEMAS, SCRIPTS, DELTACTS and THEMES we can develop a metaphor to show how ideas may be generated and the role that creative problem-solving aids can play in helping the ideas to emerge. I refer to this as 'the index metaphor' (see Figure 3.12).

This supposes that we store all our information and experience in a huge 'mental book' which has an index and cross-referencing facilities. How we deal with a problem is influenced by our perception of it. We take our perceived problem, identify the main THEME and look it up in an index in our memory. The index provides us with a number of references with regard to the information we have relating to the problem (SCHEMA or SCRIPTS). It may also be that we do not have any references with respect

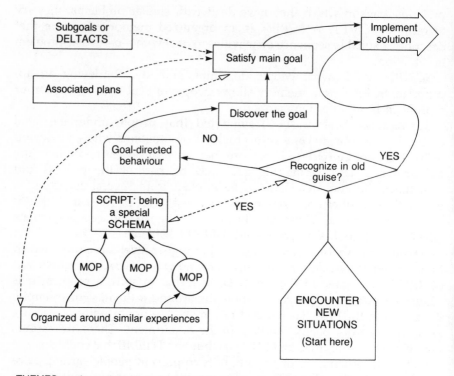

THEMES are the nucleus around which all the above are organized

Example: when finding a way of matching competition's new model of car the theme might be fuel economy

Figure 3.11 Encountering new situations and the use of SCRIPTS, GOALS, PLANS and THEMES.

to that particular problem. Assuming that there *are* such references we then look up each of these references in turn in our 'knowledge book' to see whether it provides us with the kind of information we require to solve the problem. Sometimes we may be lucky and find that a reference (the SCHEMA or SCRIPT) enables us to find an exact solution to the problem. This is either because we have previously successfully tackled and solved the same problem or because we have, at some time, learned and stored information on how to solve this particular kind of problem (an already-existing SCRIPT or SCHEMA).

At other times, when an exact fit cannot be found, there may be cross-references under the various entries in our knowledge book (MOPS) which enable us to put together sufficient information (a new SCHEMA or SCRIPT) to solve the problem. The new information (SCHEMA or SCRIPT) subsequently becomes embedded in memory for future reference.

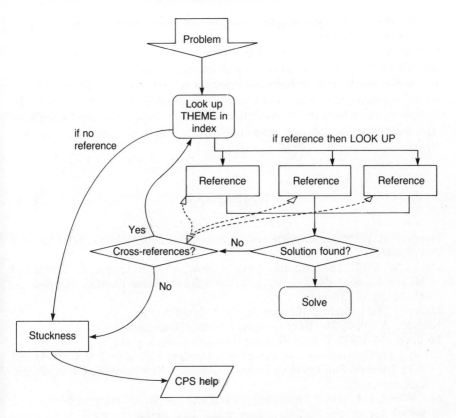

Figure 3.12 The index metaphor.

In order to do this, however, we need to know exactly what it is we are trying to achieve in terms of solving the problem (the main GOAL) and what constraints (DELTACTS) we are working under.

The 'knowledge book' is, of course, being constantly updated with new material and adjustments made to the index. New cross-references (MOPS) are also entered. A cross-reference (MOP) may be entered every time two apparently unrelated, weakly related or unrelated events seem to have a bearing on a particular matter. The cross-references (MOPS) may fade with time if they are not subsequently reinforced with evidence to support their usefulness.

Working through our 'knowledge book' enables us to solve many of the problems we encounter. Moreover, the speed of access through the index can be very fast indeed. However, there are two occasions when use of the 'knowledge book' may fail us. In the first instance we may be unable to find any entry in the index which is helpful. Secondly, the complexities of the cross-references may be so large that they exceed the capabilities of our information-processing capacity. In either case we may become stuck with a problem.

It is at this point that creative problem-solving aids can be extremely useful. They force us to look up entries in our 'knowledge book' which we would not normally consider relevant in our search of the index and for which there are either no existing recognizable cross-references in the entries or for which the cross-entries are so far down the line of 'looking up' that it would take an immense amount of time and effort to find them.

References

Hayes, J. R. (1989) *The Complete Problem Solver*, 2nd edn, Hillsdale, NJ: Lawrence Erlbaum.

Henle, M. (1962) 'The birth and death of ideas', in H. E. Gruber, G. Terrell and M. Wertheimer (eds), *Contemporary Approaches to Creative Thinking*, Symposium, University of Colorado.

Henry, J. (1991) *Creative Management*, ch. 1, London: Sage.

Koestler, A. (1967) *The Act of Creation*, London: Hutchinson.

Le Boeuf, M. (1990) *Creative Thinking*, London: Piatkus, p. 10.

Locke, J. (1690) 'An essay concerning human understanding', in J. V. Canfield and F. H. Donnell, *Readings in the Theory of Knowledge*, East Norwalk, CT: Appleton-Century-Crofts.

McClelland, J. L. (1981) 'Retrieving general and specific information from stored knowledge of specifics', *Proceedings of the Third Annual Meeting of the Cognitive Science Society*, pp. 170–2.

McClelland, J. L. and Rumelhart, D. E. (1986) 'A distributed model of human learning and memory', in D. E. Rumelhart, J. L. McClelland and the PDP Research Group (eds), *Parallel Distributed Processing, Vol. 2: Psychological and Biological Models*, Cambridge, Mass.: MIT Press.

Perkins, D. (1981) *The Mind's Best Work*, Cambridge, Mass.: Harvard University Press.

Poincaré, H. (1952) *Science and Man*, trans. F. Maitland, New York: Dover Publications.

Quillian, M. R. (1968) 'Semantic memory', in M. Minsky (ed.), *Semantic Information Processing*, Cambridge, Mass: MIT Press.

Rickards, T. (1988) *Creativity and Innovation: A Transatlantic Perspective, Creativity and Innovation Yearbook*, Vol. 1, Manchester Business School, pp. 69–77.

Rumelhart, D. E. and Norman, D. A. (1983) *Representation in Memory*, CHIP Technical Report, No. 116, San Diego: Center for Human Information Processing, University of California.

Schank, R. and Abelson, R. (1977) *Scripts, Plans, Goals and Understanding: An enquiry into human knowledge structures*, Hillsdale, NJ: Lawrence Erlbaum.

Van Andel, M. V. (1989) *Presentation to Second European Conference on Creativity and Innovation: Learning from Practice*, Noordwijk, December.

Wallas, G. (1926) *The Art of Thought*, London: Jonathan Cape.
Weisburg, R. W. (1986) *Creativity, Genius and Other Myths*, New York: W. H. Freeman.
Wertheimer, M. (1945) *Productive Thinking*, New York: Harper & Row.
Zervos, C. (1932) *Pablo Picasso*, trans. Brewster Ghiselin, Paris: Editions Cahiers D'Art.

4

Identifying the problem

Discovering the problem is often the first stage in the process of problem solving. This is then followed by the identification of objectives that need to be fulfilled in order to find a solution to the problem. Problems are best discovered by maintaining an efficient system of environmental scanning. Such a system should operate equally with respect to both the organization's external environment and its internal environment. In the case of the external environment one needs to monitor trends in the economy, changes in the law, technological advancements, changes in customer wants and needs, changes in sociocultural patterns, competitors' activities, potential customers' activities, and so on. In the case of the internal environment attention needs to be given to employee satisfaction and grievances, performance of plant and machinery, efficiency of working practices and procedures, and so on. By having an efficient monitoring system one can even anticipate problems before they actually arise.

Problems may also be identified or highlighted by systematic search. Structuring tools such as SWOT analysis can help to pinpoint problems and suggest strategies for coping with problems. SWOT (strengths, weaknesses, opportunities and threats) analysis is a technique designed specifically to help identify suitable business strategies for an organization to follow. It involves specifying and relating both organizational strengths and weaknesses and environmental opportunities and threats.

Here we will use a variation of SWOT analysis (developed from an idea by Weihrich, 1982) to help identify factors which give rise to problems. The method helps to suggest objectives, based on strengths and weaknesses of the organization, and then to specify problems that need to be tackled in order to achieve these objectives. First, major strengths and weaknesses of the organization are identified along with the objectives that they give rise to. Next, major opportunities and threats are found.

Service: airline
Objectives based on

	Strengths 1. Build on reliability 2. Make use of large fleet	Weaknesses 1. Rejuvenate image 2. Reduce high costs
Opportunities 1. Holiday flights 2. City hoppers	How to position service on reliability in getting into city hopping (S1, O2)	How to develop new image and become involved in holiday travel (O1, W1)
Threats 1. New entrants 2. Deregulation	How to position on reliability and large fleet to meet competition from new entrants to the industry (S1, S2, T1)	How to reduce costs to stave off problems associated with new entrants to the industry and deregulation (W2, T1, T2)

Figure 4.1 Setting objectives in relationship to strengths, weaknesses, opportunities and threats.

These are then listed as shown in Figure 4.1. Two of the techniques mentioned later in the chapter, goal orientation and the Why method, can be useful in helping to identify objectives if this proves difficult.

In the example shown in Figure 4.1 the airline company identifies its main strengths and weaknesses and sets objectives with respect to how it can exploit its strengths (for example, build on reliability) and compensate for its weaknesses (for example, reduce high costs). At the same time it identifies opportunities (for example, city hoppers) and threats (for example, new entrants). By looking at combinations of strengths and opportunities, for instance, it can identify one particular problem – 'how to position its service on reliability with respect to getting into the city hopping business'. Other problems could, of course, be identified – for example, how to make use of its large fleet in exploiting the holiday flight business. Examination of the matrix shown in Figure 4.1 indicates that a number of different problems could be specified for each cell (that is, more than one problem can be described in each cell, reflecting different opportunities–threats and objectives based on strengths–weaknesses).

For each of the four cells specific problems are listed, reflecting various combinations of objectives based on strengths and opportunities, or based on weaknesses and opportunities, and so on, as shown. The next step is to ensure that the problems identified are tightly defined. In the remainder of this chapter we will look at ways of defining and redefining problems so that exact and tight definitions of problems can be achieved. The next step is to develop strategies for dealing with these problems. This is accomplished by using the various idea-generating mechanisms which are explored in subsequent chapters of the book. For example, developing a new image and becoming involved in holiday travel could involve developing joint ventures and alliances with tour operators and associating the company name with particular holiday destinations – for example, 'the airline that serves all Mediterranean destinations'.

In the above example (Figure 4.1) four problems have been identified. As has already been pointed out, using different combinations of identified SWOTs more problems could be identified. Each one of the identified problems then has to be examined, carefully, in turn. It may be that each individual problem can be redefined in a more useful and productive way.

Problem definition and redefinition

There are two important points which have to be borne in mind when trying to solve problems. The first point is that most problems can be defined in several ways so that the solutions for any given problem reflect how it has been defined. Secondly, the objectives which are being pursued serve to define a problem. For example, assuming that a firm wants to survive and flourish in an industry for many years, it may state its strategic marketing problem as 'how to sustain a long-term competitive advantage'. On the other hand, if the same firm wants to make 'quick profits' in the industry before pulling out and moving on to something else, then the problem definition would reflect such an objective. The solutions to these two problems would probably be quite different.

Another important point is that problems may not be defined clearly enough to provide a basis for finding a solution. They may be stated too vaguely or expressed at too general a level to enable workable solutions to be found. For example, simply defining a problem in terms of how to improve productivity in the organization may be much too general to find workable solutions.

Methods of problem definition or redefinition

Many of the approaches discussed under idea generation can also help to define and redefine problems. Indeed, it may often be the case that the method itself allows for problem definition or redefinition. However, there are also a number of specific techniques which are designed especially for this purpose. Whatever the case, the basic aim is to discover a new perspective on a focal problem. The reason for this is twofold. In the first instance the problem as given may have been incorrectly defined and this situation is therefore remedied through redefinitional procedures. Secondly, finding a new perspective on a problem should result in a different set of ideas being subsequently generated. Such alternative sets of ideas may be more useful than those generated without obtaining a new perspective on the problem.

There are two types of specific methods: *redefinitional* techniques and *analytical* techniques. Redefinitional techniques seek to develop a degree of remoteness from the original problem statement. In moving away from the initial perception of the problem divergent thinking is used and this may lead to more unique problem solutions. The analytical techniques, by contrast, factor a problem into its major dimensions or elements. The latter can help to organize the information available about a problem as well as provide new information.

Redefinitional techniques

To illustrate, we will consider the following four techniques:

□ Boundary examination
□ Goal orientation
□ Five Ws and Hs
□ Progressive abstractions

Boundary examination (De Bono, 1970)
The purpose of using this technique is to restructure the assumptions of a problem and so produce a new perspective on a problem (Figure 4.2). It involves the following steps:

1. An initial statement of the problem is written out.

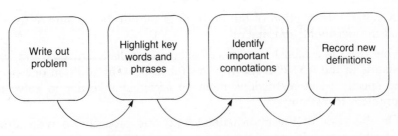

Figure 4.2 Boundary examination.

2. Important words and phrases in the statement are highlighted and examined for any hidden assumptions.

3. The important connotation of assumptions are identified, without considering the relevance of assumptions.

4. Any new problem definition implied by the implication is recorded.

Example
A firm wants to increase its sales volume and is looking for ways of doing this.

1.   In what ways might we encourage consumers to purchase our product in larger quantities?

2–3. Boundaries are examined by looking at whether responsibility might be shifted from the company to the consumer; for example, whether consumers might be rewarded rather than just encouraged to purchase the product, or even punished in some way for not buying it; and whether attention might better be given to using rather than buying.

4.   Might be redefined as: how might customers be rewarded for buying our product in larger quantities?

There is no doubt that boundary examination can produce thought-provoking problem definitions. However, there are no clear guidelines for suggesting how boundary assumptions should be analyzed.

Goal orientation (Rickards, 1974)
As the name of the technique implies, the main purpose of this technique is to provide a way of thinking about a problem in order to clarify its goals or objectives. As such it is a useful method to employ at the objective-finding stage of the creative problem-solving process (Figure 4.3). In fact, it can be a critical problem-solving activity. The technique involves the following:

1. A general description of the problem is set out, being sure to include all the pertinent information.

2. One seeks to establish what needs to be accomplished (needs) and what stands in the way of achieving this (obstacles). In addition one needs to specify what restrictions must be accepted in order to solve the problem (constraints).

3. On the basis of the information in (2) one proceeds to write down possible redefinitions of the original problem statement.

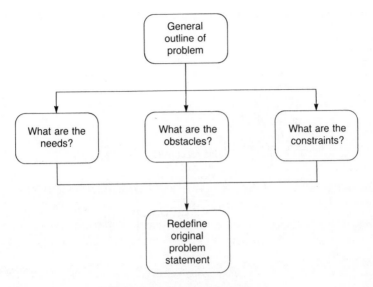

Figure 4.3 Goal orientation.

Example

1. Workers in a factory in a depressed part of England are concerned that the work will disappear during the recession and that they will lose their jobs.
2. *Need* – keep jobs safe from the impact of recession.
   Constraint – steady flow of orders from outside.
   Obstacle – bargaining power is weak during recession.
3. How to keep the job, although they have a weak bargaining position and the flow of orders is intermittent.

Note: one possible solution might be to involve workers in trying jointly to find out ways of riding the recession.

Five Ws and H
The six honest serving men method (Parnes, Noller and Biondi, 1977) is known as the 'Five Ws and H approach'. The technique has its origins in journalism, where such questions assist writers to gather story data in a systematic fashion. The technique is useful at the fact-finding stage of the creative problem-solving process, although it can also be applied usefully at other stages. The main purpose of the technique is to provide a framework for systematically gathering data relevant to a problem. Such

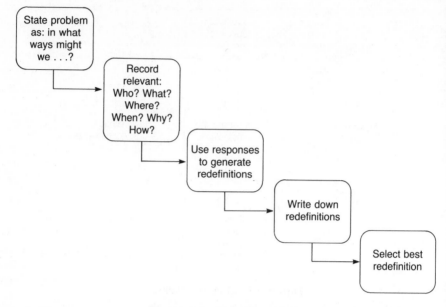

Figure 4.4 Five Ws and H.

data can enable new perspectives on a problem to be obtained, which in turn can lead to problem redefinition. The steps are as follows:

1. The problem is stated in the format: In what ways might . . .? (IWWM . . .? see Figure 4.4).
2. Separate lists of Who? What? Where? When? Why? and How? questions relevant to the general problem are then written down. During this process all judgement is withheld.
3. The responses to each question are examined and used as stimuli to generate problem redefinitions.
4. Any redefinitions which result from (3) are recorded.
5. One redefinition that seems best to reflect the problem that is to be resolved is selected.

Example
The problem concerns stoppages and disputes occurring in government departments.

1. IWWM we prevent industrial disputes from happening?
2. Who are the people concerned?

Answer: White collar workers who are not satisfied with their terms and conditions of employment.

Who are not satisfied?
Answer: Those without direct supervision; those who think they are underpaid.

What is satisfaction?
Answer: That which provides the conditions to facilitate action and accomplishment in the workplace.

What motivates most employees?
Answer: Feelings of achievement, etc.

Where are employees motivated to work hard?
Answer: In their work areas, etc.

Where is employee dissatisfaction not a problem?
Answer: Where basic personal and work needs are taken care of, etc.

When are employees dissatisfied?
Answer: When they feel their contributions are not recognized and appreciated; when they do not have adequate resources to do their jobs; when their bosses are overbearing; when their co-workers are uncooperative.

When do bosses try to create employee satisfaction?
Answer: During scheduled performance evaluations; when employees make a mistake; when employees do something well; when they are under pressure to increase productivity.

Why create employee satisfaction?
Answer: To increase productivity; to increase personal income due to employee participation in profit sharing; to become more competitive with other companies.

How can employees be satisfied?
Answer: With rewards; by being asked what they want and need to do their job better.

This might lead to the following:

IWWM we change perceptions about terms and conditions of employment?

IWWM we provide certain employees with more direct supervision?

IWWM we reward employees?

IWWM we establish more realistic employee work goals?

IWWM we better provide resources employees need to do their jobs?

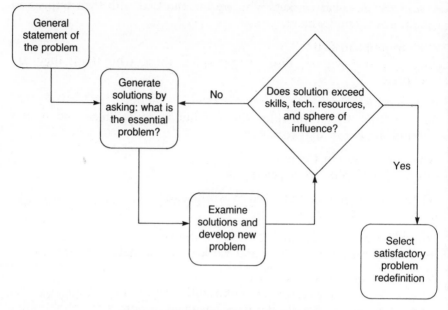

Figure 4.5 Progressive abstractions.

IWWM we better meet employees' basic needs?

IWWM we enrich employee jobs?

IWWM we involve employees in determining how to do their jobs?

IWWM we increase the company's overall productivity?

IWWM we increase cooperation among employees?

The technique can produce a number of different new problem perspectives, some of which may even enable the problem to be resolved.

Progressive abstractions

This technique (Geschka, Schaude and Schlicksupp, 1973) produces different problem definitions by employing progressively higher levels of problem abstraction until a satisfactory definition of a problem is achieved (Figure 4.5). At this higher level of abstraction it may be easier to identify possible solutions.

It is a method which relies on repeatedly trying to identify the essential problem through a series of abstractions from problem redefinitions. The steps are:

1. A general statement of the problem is written down.

2. Possible problem solutions are generated by asking the question: what is the essential problem?

3. New problem definitions are developed from the answers produced at (2).

4. (2) and (3) are repeated until the solutions begin to exceed existing skills and technological resources and/or until the solutions are outside one's sphere of influence.

5. A satisfactory problem definition is chosen and used as a basis for generating new ideas.

Example
The problem is concerned with improving the effectiveness of the sales force. At each abstraction there may be more than one possible solution or problem definition.

1. To improve the effectiveness of the sales force.

2. IWWM we improve sales force effectiveness?

3. (a) employ more sales people;
   (b) change the compensation scheme;
   (c) improve selection procedures when hiring sales staff.

4. IWWM we change the compensation scheme?

   (a) higher commissions;
   (b) commission only.

5. IWWM we use commission only?

   (a) fixed percentage of sales;
   (b) fixed percentage of sales varying across different goods.

6. IWWM we relate percentage commissions to goods?

   (a) difficulty in selling goods;
   (b) amount of time required to sell goods;
   (c) profit margin on goods.

The abstractions are continued until either a working solution or number of solutions can be found or until answers seem to be impractical.

The Why method
One of the simplest of approaches to problem redefinition, again relying on changing the level of abstraction, is the Why method (Parnes, 1981). By accepting the level of abstraction initially presented with the problem only a limited perspective on the problem can be obtained. In changing

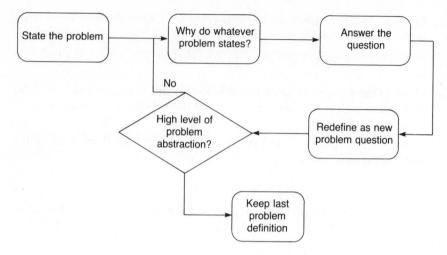

Figure 4.6 The Why method.

the level of abstraction new perspectives emerge, which in turn may lead to workable solutions being found (Figure 4.6).

In using this method one has to do the following:

1. The problem, as initially defined, is stated.
2. One asks why it is that one wants to do whatever is stated in the problem.
3. The question posed in (2) has to be answered.
4. The answer is redefined as a new problem question.
5. (2) and (3) are repeated until a high level of problem abstraction is achieved.

Example

IWWM we reduce employee absenteeism?

Question: Why do we want to reduce employee absenteeism?
Answer: To maintain adequate staffing levels.
Redefinition: IWWM we maintain adequate staffing levels?

Question: Why do we want to maintain adequate staffing levels?
Answer: So that work output levels can be maintained.
Redefinition: IWWM we ensure that work output levels are maintained?

Question: Why do we want to maintain work output levels?
Answer: To increase company profits.
Redefinement: IWWM we increase company profits?

Question: Why do we want to increase company profits?
Answer: To improve the national economy.
Redefinement: IWWM we improve the national economy?

The Why method is useful in widening out a problem and exploring its various boundaries. The method also helps the user to appraise basic goals and objectives.

Analytical techniques

Here we will consider five techniques:

☐ decomposable matrices;

☐ dimensional analysis;

☐ input–output;

☐ organized random search; and

☐ relevance systems.

Decomposable matrices (Simon, 1969)
The subjects of problems that can be viewed as complex hierarchic systems can be analyzed by breaking them down into their various subsystems (Figure 4.7). The process involves the following:

1. It is first established whether the problem is analyzable using subsystems.
2. The major subsystems and their components are enumerated.
3. A matrix of the subsystems and their components is produced.
4. Use is made of a 5-point scale to weight the degree of relationship for each of the interactions between and within the subsystems.
5. The highest-weighted interactions are selected for further analysis or generation of ideas.

Example

1. *Problem*: how to improve employee motivation within an organization.

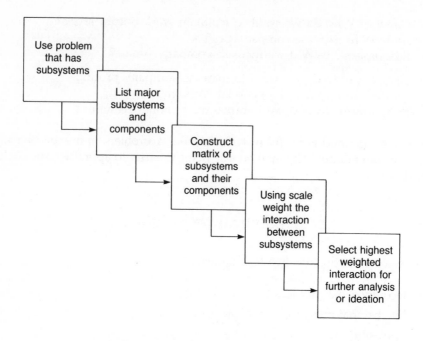

Figure 4.7   Decomposable matrices.

2. The three major subsystems are:

Organizational   (A)
Group   (B)
Individual   (C)

3.

	Organization			Group			Individual		
	A1	A2	A3	B1	B2	B3	C1	C2	C3
A1 System design		5	3	2	4	1	1	1	1
A2 Organizational Goals			4	3	2	1	1	1	1
A3 Power				3	2	3	1	1	1
B1 Leadership					4	5	3	2	4
B2 Communication						4	3	2	4
B3 Cohesiveness							4	1	4
C1 Needs								5	5
C2 Values									5
C3 Expectations									

Note: High numbers reflect greater importance of interaction.

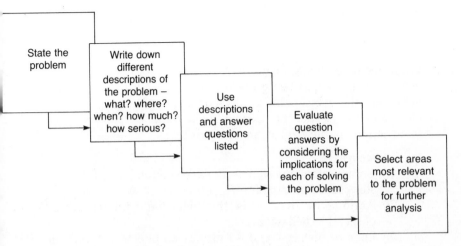

Figure 4.8 Dimensional analysis.

4. Select A1–A2, B1–B3, C1–C2, C2–C3, C1–C3, since these have the highest scores attached to them. In this example the interfaces of interest are between:

System design and organizational goals
Group leadership and communication
Individual needs and individual values
Individual values and individual expectations
Individual needs and individual expectations

and are all seen as key areas for further exploration.

Dimensional analysis (Jensen, 1978)
This is a method devised to explain and explore the dimensions and limits of a problem. It examines five elements of a problem: substantive, spatial, temporal, quantitative and qualitative (Figure 4.8). The procedure to be adopted is:

1. The problem is stated.

2. Separate descriptions of the problem in terms of What? Where? When? How much? How serious? are written down.

3. With the use of these descriptions, answers are found for questions listed for each of the dimensions (see example).

4. The answers to these questions are evaluated by assessing the significance of each for solving the problem.

5. Those areas most pertinent to the problem are selected for further analysis.

Example

1. The needs of customers are being neglected.

2. What needs are being neglected?
   Where are the needs being neglected?
   When are the needs being neglected?
   How much neglection of needs is involved?
   How serious is the neglection of needs?

3. (a) *Substantive*
     (i) Commission/omission – does something need to be done, stopped or modified?
     (ii) Attitude or deed – is the behaviour due to attitudes or observable behaviour?
     (iii) Ends or means – is it a cause or an effect?; a symptom of an underlying problem?
     (iv) Active or passive – is it threatening or just irritating?
     (v) Visible or invisible – is the real problem apparent?
   (b) *Spatial*
     (i) Local or distant – is it limited to a local geographical area?
     (ii) Particular locations within a location – can it be isolated?
     (iii) Isolated or widespread – how extensive is it?
   (c) *Temporal*
     (i) Long-standing or recent – how long has the problem been around? If solved will this lead to more problems?
     (ii) Present or impending – does it exist now, or how soon will it arise? Can it develop into something more serious?
     (iii) Constant or ebb and flow – does it occur all the time or just from time to time? Is there a pattern?
   (d) *Quantitative*
     (i) Single or multiple – are the causes one or many?
     (ii) Many or few people – how many people are involved?
     (iii) General or specific – does it apply generally or only to certain subgroups?
     (iv) Simple or complex – does it comprise only a single element or is it made up of many interlocking elements?
     (v) Affluence or scarcity – is it due to an abundance or scarcity of something?
   (e) *Qualitative*
     (i) Philosophical or surface – is the problem deep-rooted?
     (ii) Survival or enrichment – is it a matter of survival or does it merely bring into question the quality of a situation?
     (iii) Primary or secondary – is it perceived to be of primary importance?

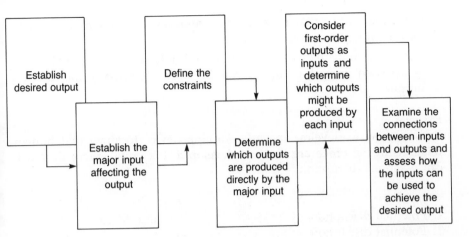

Figure 4.9 Input–output.

(iv) What values are being violated – what is wrong?

(v) To what degree are the values being violated – is it serious or trivial?

(vi) Proper or improper values – should the values be honoured?

While the method is useful in problem solving one of its best uses is as a checklist for use during pre-problem solving or as a general direction prefacing the use of some other analytic method. The checklist can help to provide a general perspective during the later stages of the problem-solving process.

Input–output technique

The input–output technique (General Electric Company) should prove useful for specifying connections between the elements of a variety of complex, dynamic problems (Figure 4.9). Potential application areas include: social planning and human relations. The usual steps involved in this form of analysis are:

1. The desired output is first established.

2. The major input affecting the output is established.

3. Any limiting specifications that the output must meet are established.

4. The outputs which are produced directly by the major input are determined.

5. First-order outputs are considered as inputs and it is determined which outputs might be produced by each input.
6. The connections between the inputs and outputs are examined and it is assessed how the inputs can be used to achieve the desired output.

Example
Problem: how to develop an early warning device to show that human relations in the office are likely to develop to the point where they will cause serious disruption.

Input	*Output*
1. Potential disruption	Warning device
2. Potential disruption	→
Disagreements/arguments	→
Written communication over trivia	

Monitor amount of written communication over trivia.

Organized random search
Organized random search was developed by Frank Williams (1960). He argued that rather than randomly searching for ideas it is better, first, to decompose a problem into its different subdivisions or parts (Figure 4.10).

1. The problem is examined for possible ways of categorizing parts of the problem.
2. The different subdivisions are noted and used to generate ideas.

Example
How to buy time when negotiating a deal. Two areas are shown in Table 4.1.

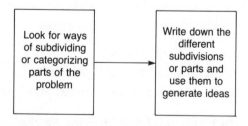

Figure 4.10 Organized random search.

Table 4.1 Organized random speech

(a) People	(b) Things
(1) Internal aspects 　　superiors 　　subordinates (2) External aspects 　　customers 　　suppliers 　　competitors	(1) Internal aspects (2) External aspects

Relevance systems

Relevance systems (Rickards, 1974) facilitate organizing information about a problem through successive refinement of the major elements of a problem. There are two types of relevance system, single and binary. A single system comprises all the elements related to a single problem. A binary system is comprised of two single systems that interact across the lower levels of the systems (the opportunity interface) (Figure 4.11). The steps are as follows:

1. The highest-order element of the problem is written down.
2. The subelements that can be derived from the first level (the second level elements) are listed.
3. Lower-level elements are enumerated until all possible levels have been exhausted and the lowest level is reached. The last situation can usually be recognized by looking for elements that answer the question: How? Higher-level elements, in contrast, answer the question: Why?
4. On completion the system's validity is assessed by working upward from the lower-level elements.
5. The lower-level elements are used to suggest possible problem solutions.
6. Should there be an overlap between the problem and another area and the two need to be integrated, the system should be extended by making a second system so that its lower-level elements interface with the first system. This will result in the creation of a binary relevance system.
7. Look at the interface to discover points of singular or mutual overlap and to consider possible constraining factors that might affect the objectives declared within either system.

Example
Problem: how to improve a company's promotional strategy (Table 4.2).

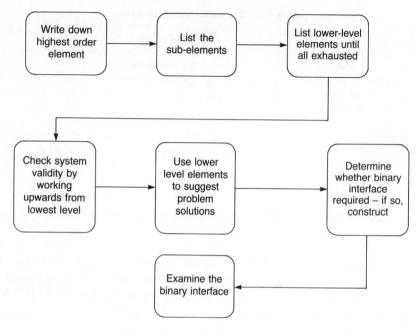

Figure 4.11 Relevance systems.

Table 4.2 Binary relevance system

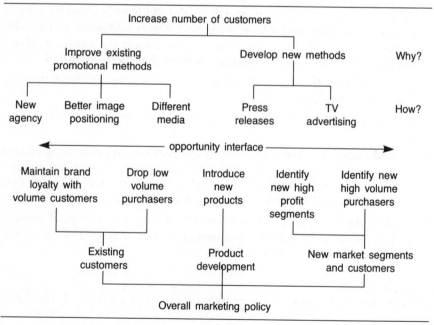

At the opportunity interface we see the possibility of using different media and identifying new high profit segments or using TV advertising in conjunction with identifying new high volume purchasers.

References

De Bono, E. (1970) *Lateral Thinking: Creativity step by step*, New York: Harper & Row.

Geschka, H., Schaude, G. R. and Schlicksupp, H. (1973) 'Modern techniques for solving problems', *Chemical Engineering*, August, 91–7.

Jensen, J. V. (1978) 'A heuristic for the analysis of the nature and extent of a problem', *Journal of Creative Behaviour*, **12**, 268–80.

Parnes, S. J. (1981) *The Magic of Your Mind*, Buffalo, NY: The Creative Education Foundation in association with Bearly Ltd.

Parnes, S. J., Noller, R. B. and Biondi, A. M. (1977) *Guide to Creative Action*, New York: Scribner.

Rickards, T. (1974) *Problem Solving Through Creative Analysis*, Aldershot: Gower.

Simon, H. A. (1969) *The Science of the Artificial*, Cambridge, Mass.: MIT Press.

Weihrich, H. (1982) 'The TOWS matrix: a tool for situational analysis', *Long Range Planning*, **15**(2), 54–66.

Williams, F. E. (1960) *Foundations of Creative Problem Solving*, Ann Arbor, MI: Edward Bros.

5

Morphological analysis and related techniques

This chapter examines a number of techniques that essentially rely on identifying attributes of a problem and structuring the problem along several dimensions to provide insights into its nature. The techniques considered are:

- Listing
- Checklists
- Clichés, proverbs and maxims
- Attribute listing
- Morphological analysis
- SCIMITAR
- Heuristic ideation technique
- Component detailing
- Allen morphologizer
- Sequence–attribute modification matrix

These techniques can be used for a wide range of problems.

Listing

This technique is often used to produce new product ideas – although it is applicable to a wide range of problems (see Whiting, 1958) (Figure 5.1). The steps involved in carrying out the method are as follows:

1. The problem is stated in concise terms.
2. A subject area which has general relevance to the problem is identified. Next, a list of all the objects, products or ideas that are related to the subject area are written down, assigning a consecutive number to each one.
3. All the items on the list generated in (2) are studied in pairs until all possible combinations are exhausted. Free association is used to develop ideas suggested by the pair under review.
4. The best combinations are selected for further evaluation.

Example
Imagine the problem is how to meet a new competitor's entry to a market with a fast-moving consumer product selling in supermarkets. Marketing is taken as the subject of general relevance to the problem. Next, various aspects of marketing are written down:

1. Selling
2. Sales promotion

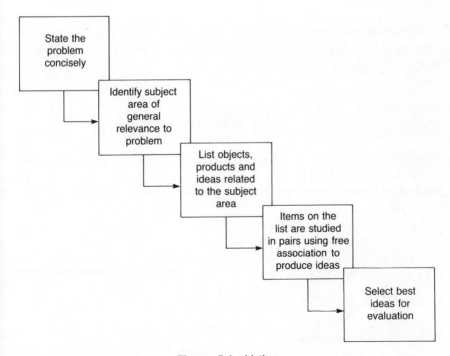

Figure 5.1 Listing.

3. Retailers

4. Customers

5. Sales people

6. Price

7. Marketing research

8. Merchandising

9. Advertising

10. New product introduction

11. Innovation in distribution, etc.

The next step is to examine items on the list in pairs. For instance:

1 and 2 – Selling and sales promotion: this might suggest a 'blitz selling' campaign in specifically targeted areas offering prizes (holidays, for example) to sales staff who achieve given targets.

10 and 11 – New products and innovative distribution: this combination may suggest bringing a new product to the market quickly (assuming this is possible) and marketing it through non-traditional distribution channels.

Novelty or richness in terms of problem solution is unlikely to emerge from this kind of approach. On the other hand, it does produce solutions that are directly pertinent to the problem.

Checklists

Checklists can be used to generate ideas and they are particularly useful for identifying new product ideas by making alterations to existing products (Taylor, 1961). A typical checklist involves considering such things as:

☐ adding or subtracting something;

☐ changing the colour;

☐ varying the materials;

☐ rearranging the parts;

☐ varying the shapes;

☐ changing the size; and

☐ modifying the design or the style.

Example
Watches:

☐ have had compasses added to them;
☐ have been combined with calculators;
☐ have been produced in many different colours;
☐ have been produced in steel, gold, silver, plastic, etc.
☐ have been produced in skeleton form so that the mechanism can be viewed;
☐ have been produced as oblongs, ovals, circles and even in the shape of a guitar; range from quite tiny to quite large;
☐ have been driven by mechanical devices (clockwork), quartz – electrical battery power, quartz – light-powered, quartz – dynamo-powered, and even water-powered.

Using checklists is very easy and they help to prevent 'overlooking' an obvious solution to a problem. Moreover, they are extremely valuable in enabling previous solutions to be adapted to current problems. Used in conjunction with other more open-ended techniques, they can be quite productive.

Clichés, proverbs and maxims

Van Gundy (1993) suggests that as a variation on the checklist approach one can make use of clichés, proverbs and maxims as unrelated idea stimuli (Figure 5.2). The steps are as follows:

1. A proverb, cliché or maxim that is attractive to the user(s) and which has no obvious associations with the problem is chosen.
2. A note of any interpretations and implications of the chosen phrase or sentence is made without reference to the problem.
3. The implications and references obtained in (2) are used to stimulate ideas with respect to the original problem.
4. Another proverb, maxim or cliché is chosen and (2–4) are repeated until a satisfactory solution is obtained.

Example
Problem: how to recruit better quality clerical staff.

1. *Stimulus*: an apple a day keeps the doctor away.

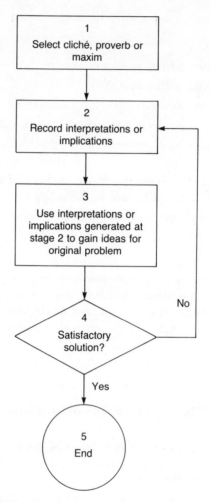

Figure 5.2 Clichés, proverbs and maxims.

2. (a) Eating apples keeps one well.
   (b) Apples are health-giving.
   (c) Doctor's visits occur when one is sick.
   (d) Regular healthy eating assures a healthy existence.

3. Useful interpretations for the original problem: regular recruitment exercises may produce a steady flow of good quality clerical grade personnel.

1. *Stimulus*: you can't tell a book by its cover.

2. Covers are to gain people's interest in a book and do not necessarily reflect content, nor what something is really made of.

3. Appearances are deceptive.

Implications for the original problem
Both (2) and (3) indicate that one needs to study applications for posts in some depth. Judging by short interviews and on the basis of fleeting impressions is to be avoided.

Van Gundy (1993) lists 25 top-rated items according to their ability to evoke visual images. The top 10 are:

1. When the cat's away the mouse will play.
2. The early bird catches the worm.
3. Like father, like son.
4. Kill two birds with one stone.
5. Don't count your chickens before they're hatched.
6. If the shoe fits wear it.
7. Monkey see, monkey do.
8. A man's home is his castle.
9. The bigger they are, the harder they fall.
10. Birds of a feather flock together.

Attribute listing

Attribute listing as a creative problem-solving technique was mentioned by Crawford (1954) (Figure 5.3). It is perhaps best illustrated with an example. Suppose a company want to come up with ideas for a new toothbrush. A first step would be to list the attributes of the existing model. For example:

☐ made of plastic;
☐ manually operated;
☐ needs a supply of water and toothpaste.

The next step involves taking each attribute in turn and considering how it might be improved.

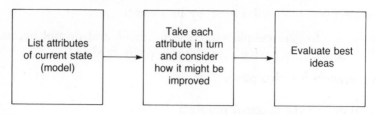

Figure 5.3 Attribute listing.

Made of plastic

☐ could it be made in other materials?
☐ could it be made more cheaply in other materials?
☐ could it be made of 'green' materials?
☐ disposable, throwaway material?

Operation

☐ Manually operated?
☐ Electrically or mechanically operated?

Needs a supply of water and toothpaste

☐ Could these be included in the design?

All the best ideas are taken forward for evaluation.

One difficulty with the method is that it is relatively easy to become caught up on attributes that are not really essential to the product or problem. One should concentrate upon those attributes related to primary functions. It is advisable to have no more than seven attributes under consideration at a time, otherwise the number of relations between attributes can become too large and unmanageable. The technique can be somewhat restrictive in terms of ideas generated and often they may be similar to the original attributes.

Morphological analysis

Any systematic attempt to classify a system in terms of its components or forms is essentially a morphological analysis (Figure 5.4). Zwicky (1948) describes a mathematical treatment of the technique. More often, however,

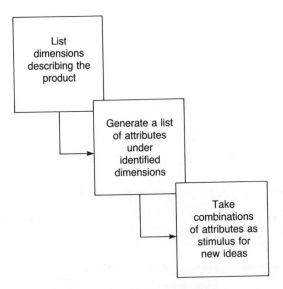

Figure 5.4 Morphological analysis.

the approach is employed in a qualitative manner, in order to assist in a systematic search of a complex problem or system. The technique has been used in many contexts, including product design, technological innovation, market research and social problems analysis.

The approach involves, first, listing the possible dimensions that together describe a problem or system being studied. For example, if one was trying to identify possible new product ideas then one might consider such things as the shape of the product and the material from which it is made as two such dimensions. While any number of dimensions can be used, a typical approach is to break the problem into two or three dimensions.

The next step involves generating or listing attributes under the various dimensions that have been identified. In the above example, if the type of product under consideration is a car, then under the dimension 'shape' one might list such attributes as bullet-shaped, box-shaped with wheels at each corner, etc. (see Figure 5.5). Once the listing of attributes has been exhausted one then has to examine as many combinations of attributes across the identified dimensions as possible and pick out any promising or unusual ideas; for example, a bullet-shaped car made of aluminium (aluminium and bullet-shaped having been listed under the dimensions of 'material' and 'shape', respectively). Promising ideas may be subsequently evaluated for their suitability.

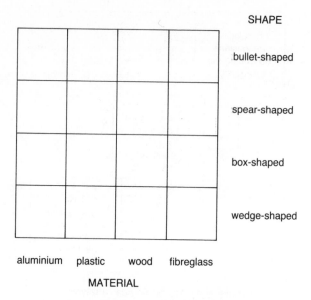

Figure 5.5 Morphological analysis.

Manual methods for undertaking morphological analysis are time consuming and extremely unwieldy. This is due mainly to the large number of combinations of attributes that can be formed. A computerized version of the technique has been produced which greatly facilitates its use (Proctor, 1989). Furthermore, the model also generates random words which can be used to suggest attributes for identified dimensions.

The technique is clearly ideal for generating a large number of ideas of an exploratory or opportunity-seeking nature. Majaro (1991) suggests that the technique is particularly useful for generating ideas about:

□ new products or services;
□ applications for new materials;
□ new market segments and applications;
□ new ways of developing a competitive advantage;
□ novel promotional techniques for products or services; and
□ identification of new location opportunities.

Where only one solution exists, where the remit is very small or, in any situation or problem which is known to have only one dimension, morphological analysis is not considered to be a suitable tool.

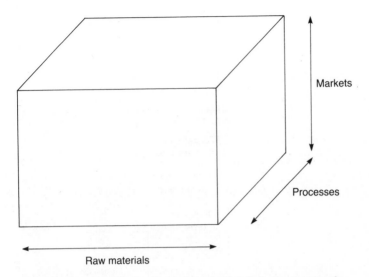

Figure 5.6 The three dimensions to the Scimitar approach.

SCIMITAR

Somewhat allied to the concept of morphological analysis is the Scimitar system developed by John Carson. In the 1980s, Carson developed a method for searching for new products (Carson and Rickards, 1979). Its idea-generation mechanism is a three-dimensional model of the company, which is systematically searched to find multiple answers to the question: market needs + corporate means = ? Scimitar has been used widely in many firms and has never failed to yield valuable new product ideas (see Figure 5.6).

Heuristic ideation technique

The technique described here provides a systematic approach to developing new product ideas and is akin to attribute listing and morphological analysis. It is developed, with modifications, from ideas suggested by Tauber (1972) concerning the heuristic ideation technique (Figure 5.7).

The method decomposes existing products into lists of factors or attributes. For example, cars might be decomposed into such factors–attributes as roof, seats, movement, and so on. Next, another product is decomposed and the two lists are then arrayed. Finally, one takes different combinations in the search for stimulation.

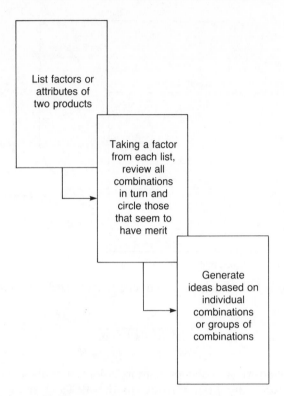

Figure 5.7   Heuristic idea generating.

In reducing the number of combinations considered, the technique makes use of two major heuristics: first, the essentials of most product ideas can be described with the aid of a two-word combination. A second heuristic might be that some combinations of factors are likely to be more interesting than others. Combinations from different categories are likely to be unique or more interesting than others.

The procedure for using the technique is as follows:

1. Construct two lists that make up two product areas. For example, one list might include car components–attributes (tyres, seats, movement, etc.) and homes (furniture, utensils, tools, entertainment, carpets, comfort, etc.). The next step is to assign a number to each possible combination. For example, the combination of tyres and furniture might be assigned 1, tyres and tools 2, etc.).

2. All the factors should then be reviewed and any two-word combination that appears to have potential or is interesting should be circled.

3. By examining individual combinations or taking groups of combinations together identify potential ideas.

Example
A firm engaged in producing kitchen tables is looking for new product ideas. Two products are taken and decomposed into factors:

Product	*Factors*
kitchen tables	legs, top, size
deck-chairs	collapsible, portable, frame, canvas

Various combinations are listed and numbered:

1. legs: collapsible
2. legs: portable
3. legs: frame
4. legs: canvas
5. top: collapsible
6. top: portable
7. top: frame
8. top: canvas
9. size: collapsible
10. size: portable
11. size: frame
12. size: canvas

Combinations 1, 2, 5, 6, 7, 8, 9 and 10 all suggested some sort of travelling table which could be taken to picnics and barbecues. The result was a new table product with folding legs and a canvas top which could be rigidly secured when the legs were unfolded. A metal base frame provides additional rigidity (Figure 5.8).

The technique presents a systematic way of generating a relatively large quantity of possible ideas. On the other hand, it suffers from the disadvantage that not all factors may be considered in the grid. Careful attention must be given to ensure that all the relevant important factors are included. In addition, because it relies on related stimuli and forced relationships, it is a method which may not produce unique solutions.

Component detailing

This technique combines features of attribute listing and morphological analysis (Wakin, 1985) (Figure 5.9). The steps are as follows:

1. Working as a team the group members list the major components of the problem.

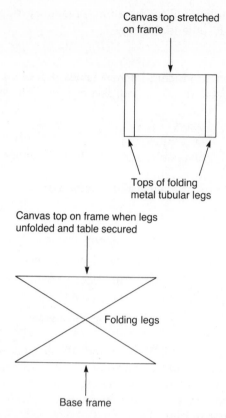

Figure 5.8 Canvas top, folding, portable table.

2. The attributes of each component are identified and listed by the group.
3. Individual members of the group are given a different problem component.
4. The group member studies the component and its attributes, noting all the details.
5. Each group member draws a picture of his or her assigned component showing as much detail as possible.
6. Drawings are then collected and displayed so that they are visible to all group members. Attention should be given to displaying the pictures in a logical order.
7. The collage is examined for possible ideas.

The technique is quite useful for looking at product improvement, although many different kinds of problems can be studied. For example, suppose the problem is how to organize an away-day at which company

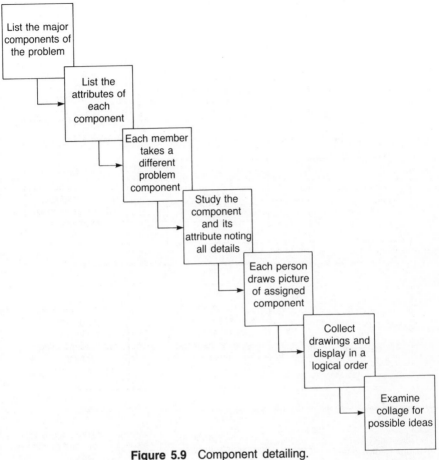

Figure 5.9 Component detailing.

strategy is to be discussed. First, the group should list all the components of the away-day, such as who is to participate, the venue, a list of topics, rooms required, meals required, and so on. The attributes of these components are listed next. Venue, for example, might be described in terms of different known locations and in terms of desirable characteristics. Next, the group members draw pictures of their components and finally the pictures are assembled to represent the problem. The pictures are then examined for idea stimulation.

The technique assists people to see a problem from new perspectives by using component drawings that vary in size and different drawing styles. The main weakness of the method lies in the fact that it is perhaps only really useful when one is dealing with problems that involve tangible objects. Abstract representations can, of course, be effected but this is more subjective. Representations of such a kind can, however, provide interesting stimulus to thought.

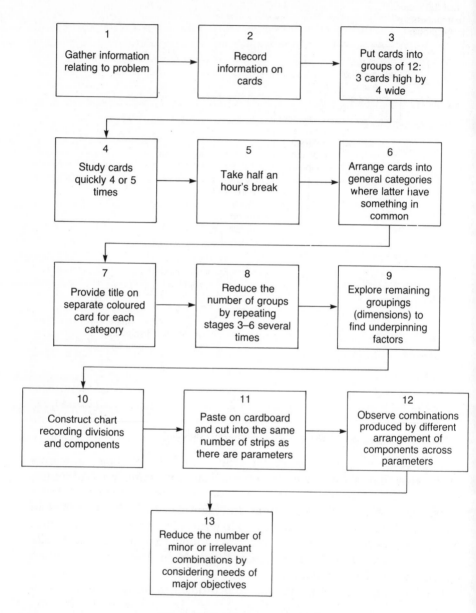

Figure 5.10 Allen morphologizer.

The Allen morphologizer

Allen (1962) refined the morphological analysis method so that it could organize and sort problem dimensions and their subdivisions. In Allen's terms a dimension is a 'parameter' and its subdivision a component (Figure 5.10). The method to adopt is as follows:

1. Collect all the information that can relate to a problem without paying attention to its importance.
2. The information should be recorded on cards (3″ wide × 2.5″ high).
3. Without paying attention to order the cards should be put into groups of 12. The cards should be arranged so that they are three cards wide × four cards high.
4. The cards should be studied quickly four or five times.
5. The exercise should be abandoned for half an hour or so and some other type of activity undertaken.
6. On returning to the cards, these should then be studied and arranged into general categories so that all the cards in one category seem to have something in common.
7. A descriptive title should be given to each category. These should be written down on separate cards using a different colour of ink. The cards should then be placed, as appropriate, next to each card group.
8. The number of groups should then be reduced by repeating steps (3–6) several times, treating the groups as units. This should be done until at least four but no more than seven groups remain. Each of the remaining groups is then considered to be a problem parameter or a 'dimension'.
9. Each of the remaining groupings should now be explored to find underpinning 'factors'. The number of identified factors should be reduced to no more than seven and are called 'components' or 'subdivisions'.
10. A chart is constructed, recording the parameters (divisions) across the top of the page with the components listed below.
11. The chart is then pasted onto a piece of cardboard and cut into the same number of vertical strips as there are parameters.
12. The strips should be placed side by side and moved slowly up and down to observe the combinations produced by different arrangements of the components across the parameters.
13. The number of irrelevant or minor combinations is reduced by

considering the needs of major objectives specified in the problem and which, if achieved, will solve the problem.

Example

Recession has depressed the market. The problem is to find a way of maintaining a competitive advantage. A group tackling this problem eventually arrived at (8), as outlined above, and identified four parameters or 'divisions':

1. Reducing costs and hence price through value engineering.
2. Maintaining market share through extensive marketing promotions.
3. Innovating in terms of distribution.
4. Adding further value to existing products by improving the augmented product – for example, improved delivery times.

At (9) the factors or components (subdivisions) identified were as shown below:

Division 1 (cost reduction)
 (i) Improved materials to make up the product.
 (ii) Cheaper materials to make up the product.
(iii) Different suppliers to facilitate (i) and (ii).

Division 2 (marketing promotions)
 (i) Improved sales promotion.
 (ii) Improved advertising.
(iii) Marketing public relations.

Division 3 (distribution innovation)
 (i) Direct marketing.
 (ii) New or additional distributors.

Division 4 (augmented product)
 (i) Improved delivery times.
 (ii) Improved after-sales service.
(iii) Improved warranty on goods supplied.

Mixing and matching the various combinations possible indicated that the following would be most likely to lead to meeting the objectives specified in the problem: improved materials (value engineering), marketing public relations, new distributors and improved warranty on goods supplied.

This technique introduces considerable structure into the problem-solving process through the development of problem dimensions and their respective subdivisions. This avoids trial and error problem solving and provides an opportunity to consider possibilities that might otherwise easily be overlooked. Clearly, as the number of problem dimensions and subdivisions increases the number of possible solutions increases geometrically and difficulty is experienced in evaluating options – which is a problem in the case of ordinary morphological analysis. The Allen variation, however, circumvents this particular problem.

Sequence–attribute modification matrix

Where a problem contains a logical sequence of steps this technique, developed by Brooks, has merit. Combining elements of attribute listing, checklists and morphological analysis, it also makes use of forced relationships to stimulate idea generation (Figure 5.11). The procedure is as follows:

1. Write down the logical steps involved in the process to which the problem relates.
2. Specify generic ways in which the process can be modified (for example, eliminate, substitute, rearrange, combine, increase, decrease, etc.).
3. Make a two-dimensional matrix in which the steps appear vertically along the left-hand edge and the modifications horizontally along the top of the matrix.
4. Study the cells of the matrix looking for changes that seem promising or that would benefit from a detailed study.
5. Suggest ideas for making the modifications.

Example
Problem: inability to convert sales interviews into actual sales.

1. Steps in the process
   (a) Research background of client prior to making call.
   (b) Arrange interview by telephone.
   (c) Send literature through post prior to interview.
   (d) Attend for interview at appointed time.
   (e) Get the prospect's attention.
   (f) Develop the prospect's interest.
   (g) Arouse the prospect's desire .
   (h) Get the prospect to *act* and place an order.
   (i) Close the interview.

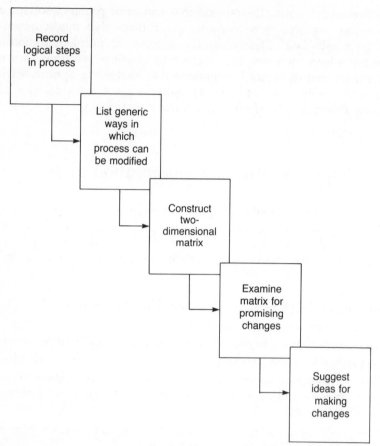

Figure 5.11   Steps in the construction of the sequence–attribute modification matrix.

    (j) Ensure that the order is fulfilled as promised.
    (k) Call back to ensure that the client is satisfied with the goods.

2. Eliminate, substitute, rearrange, combine, increase, decrease, separate, improve.

3. Construct matrix
    (a) Research client.
    (b) Arrange interview.
    (c) Send literature.
    (d) Attend interview.
    (e) Get attention.
    (f) Develop interest.
    (g) Arouse desire.

	Rearrange	Increase	Decrease	Improve
1. Research client		X		
2. Arrange interview	X			
3. Send literature				X
4. Attend interview				
5. Get attention		X		
6. Develop interest				X
7. Arouse desire				X
8. Get action				X
9. Close interview				X
10. Ensure delivery			X	
11. Check client satisfaction		X		

Figure 5.12 Two-dimensional grid.

(h) Get action.

(i) Close interview.

(j) Ensure delivery.

(k) Check client satisfaction.

4. Construct a two-dimensional grid (Figure 5.12).

5. Observations

    (a) More time might be spent researching the client so that better information is available upon which to base the sales interview. Alternatively, support staff at the office might be able to provide backup.

    (b) The interview might be arranged so that it coincides with the best time for the prospect. Poor timing of interviews is a major cause of unsuccessful sales calls.

    (c) The quality and relevance of the sales literature sent to prospects might be improved substantially. Better research at (a) will indicate the kind of literature that the client will want.

    (d) Point (e), getting attention – efforts might be made to increase the speed with which attention is gained since this is the initial stage in the sales process. If attention is not gained early in the interview it may never be obtained.

    (e) Points (f)–(i) – developing interest, arousing desire, getting action and closing the interview. These all relate to the quality of the sales 'pitch', or sales argument. Improvement of quality is what is required. This may amount to improving general sales technique or to specific product, company or client knowledge.

    (f) Ensuring delivery (j) is part of the salesperson's job. If delivery is late then the customer will be dissatisfied and not only will he or she be less inclined to place an order at a subsequent interview, but he or she may also influence other customers. The aim here is to decrease any delays in the delivery system.

(g) Check client satisfaction (k). The argument here is that it is important to establish that the customer is satisfied with the goods that are delivered. That is, the goods should perform as specifications indicate. The salesperson has to increase the level of the client's satisfaction and this is done by sorting out any major or minor problems that arise once the goods are being used.

This technique is extremely useful where the problem lies in a process. It cannot, however, be applied to problems which are not contained in processes.

References

Allen, M. S. (1962) *Morphological Creativity*, Englewood Cliffs, NJ: Prentice Hall.

Brooks, J. D. *Review of Operational Mechanisms for Innovative Management Course*, Pittsburgh, PA: Industrial Studies program, US Steel Corporation.

Carson, J. W. and Rickards, T. (1979) *Industrial New Product Development*, Aldershot: Gower.

Crawford, R. P. (1954) *The Techniques of Creative Thinking*, Englewood Cliffs, NJ: Prentice Hall.

Majaro, S. (1991) *The Creative Marketer*, Oxford: Butterworth Heinemann.

Proctor, R. A. (1989) 'Innovations in new product screening and evaluation', *Technology Analysis and Strategic Management*, 1(3), 313–24.

Tauber, E. M. (1972) 'HIT: heuristic ideation technique – a systematic procedure for new product search', *Journal of Marketing*, 36, 58–61.

Taylor, J. W. (1961) *How to Create Ideas*, Englewood Cliffs, NJ: Prentice Hall.

Van Gundy, A. B. (1988) *Techniques of Structured Problem Solving*, New York: Van Nostrand Reinhold.

Wakin, E. (1985) 'Component detailing', Presentation at the 31st Annual Creative Problem Solving Institute, Buffalo, NY: June.

Whiting, C. S. (1958) *Creative Thinking*, New York: Van Nostrand Reinhold.

Zwicky, F. (1948) *Discovery Invention Research Through the Morphological Approach*, New York: Macmillan.

6

Brainstorming and its variants

There is little doubt that brainstorming is the most well known and used of all group creative problem-solving techniques. The term 'brainstorm' itself comes from the idea of using the brain to storm a problem. There are many variants of the techniques and we examine some of these variants in this chapter. In principle, a brainstorming session is simply a creative meeting at which a list of ideas is produced for subsequent evaluation and processing as solutions to problems.

Brainstorming is a very effective technique and its success owes much to the dynamics of the group situation. Whenever a person shouts out a new idea that person stirs not only his or her own imagination but everyone else's as well. Brainstorming starts a chain reaction of associations in everyone's minds and this is a prime cause of the technique's effectiveness. It is also argued that a brainstorming session constitutes a social process at which individuals tend to think up more ideas than they would if they were left to do so on their own. This may be partly due to motivational factors, in that they have to compete with others to think up ideas. Another point is that all ideas are accepted by the group and none are rejected. This is in strong contrast with conventional business meetings where hostility to others' viewpoints may be expressed. Where hostility is expressed concerning a participant's views that person may feel less willing to keep putting forward ideas. In the brainstorming session, however, having ideas accepted spurs one to come up with more ideas.

Brainstorming was conceived originally as a complete problem-solving process. In other words, it was the intention that the method would enable one to deal with several of the creative problem-solving stages. The brainstorming process permits redefining of the problem, generating ideas, finding possible solutions, developing feasible solutions and evaluating solutions.

Classical brainstorming

Osborn (1953) is often credited with being the inventor of brainstorming as a technique that helps to overcome the restrictive nature of evaluation that takes place in most business meetings. Osborn believed that social pressures inhibited individuals from stating their ideas and he set about trying to remedy this situation through the medium of structured meetings, at which ideas were to be freely expressed prior to evaluation.

Osborn felt that the approach was one anyone could use whenever searching for ideas. He advocated the virtue of 'deferment of judgement' as an aid to creativity. Later work at Buffalo in the United States, by Parnes (1963), supported Osborn's claims that through the deferment of judgement principle more and more good ideas could be produced in unit time.

One of the basic principles behind brainstorming is the deferment of critical judgement and the spontaneous presentation to the group of any ideas that occur to any person in the group. The procedure is used to facilitate divergent thinking and the production of many ideas. It is not used to produce convergent thinking, nor does it provide the answer to a problem that has a single solution.

Osborn had four basic rules for brainstorming:

1. Criticism is not permitted – adverse judgement of ideas must be withheld. No one should criticize anyone else's ideas.

2. Free-wheeling is welcome – the wilder the idea the better. One should not be afraid to say anything that comes into one's mind – the stranger the idea the better. This complete freedom stimulates more and better ideas.

3. Quantity is required – the greater the number of ideas, the more likelihood of winners. One should try to come up with as many ideas as possible.

4. Combinations and improvements should be tried out. In addition to contributing ideas of one's own, one should suggest how ideas of others can be turned into better ideas, or how two or more ideas can be joined into a still better idea.

One of the most popular forms of brainstorming takes the form of a group activity. A warm-up session is advocated in the case where participants have not had previous experience of the technique. A group leader records all the ideas generated during the session on a flip-chart. The group members are invited to call out ideas relating to the problem as they occur: the aim is to generate as many ideas as possible – the wilder the ideas the better. Ideas are never evaluated during the generation process. By being able to see other people's ideas recorded other individuals are able to find new combinations or 'hitchhike or free-wheel' on those ideas to produce new insights.

Brainstorming as a technique dates back to before the present century. However, classical brainstorming in its current form was originally recognized and used from the early 1950s as a systematic creativity training tool. All techniques aimed at discovering new ideas and achieving a consensus by a number of people on the basis of intuitive thinking are derived from the concept of brainstorming.

Brainstorming can be carried out by individuals or by groups. It is based on the hypothesis that a large number of ideas will include at least a few good ones. However, this has not yet been proved conclusively. The basic rules for brainstorming sessions are as follows:

1. State the problem in basic terms, with only one focal point.

2. Do not find fault with, or stop to explore, any one idea.

3. Reach for any kind of idea, even if its relevance seems remote at the time.

4. Provide the support and encouragement which are so necessary to liberate participants from inhibiting attitudes.

Osborn described his method in an important and definitive text, *Applied Imagination* (1953) in which he accepted the following definition of the word 'brainstorm':

to practice a conference technique by which a group attempts to find a solution for a specific problem by amassing all the ideas spontaneously contributed by its members.

He emphasized that no conference can be called a brainstorming session unless specific rules are laid down to ensure that the idea-generation stages are separated from the evaluation stages (deferment-of-judgement principle) (Figure 6.1). He also indicated that the brainstorming session is only part of a process of creative problem solving which involved, prior to the session, a series of fact-finding and problem-defining stages, and subsequent to the session an evaluation stage which would incorporate strategy for progressing good ideas further.

Few generalizations can be made from reports of sessions on real problems in the literature as the accounts are, in general, anecdotal and incomplete. However, studies with model problems have tended to show that the underlying principle (postponement of judgement) can be used to increase the quality and number of acceptable ideas produced.

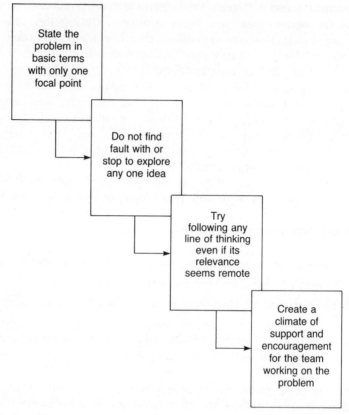

Figure 6.1 Things to bear in mind when undertaking classical brainstorming.

Main types of problem that can be tackled

Brainstorming can be used to help to find solutions to many different kinds of open-ended problems. These include:

New concepts for products or markets: new consumer product ideas for subsequent concept testing; ideas for scenarios of future markets.

Managerial problems: production of ideas for job-enrichment.

Commercialization of new technology: how to exploit a patentable discovery.

Improvements to processes: value analysis on a production operation.

Planning and trouble-shooting: anticipating scale-up difficulties; examining potential causes of unexpected machine failure.

Composition of a brainstorming group

Ideally, ·the group should be heterogeneous in background experience, skilled in the techniques and should be interested in helping without being too closely associated with the problem and with existing attitudes within the organization.

There are no clear guidelines in the literature regarding group size and it is possible that it will vary from one environment to the next, influenced by factors such as the leadership style, the individual variations developed and sheer availability of suitable participants.

Criteria for selecting participants

The less experienced the group, the less speculative the ideas and the greater the need for a large group (up to 15 people). Conversely, six participants will be sufficient if they are all experienced brainstormers.

A group of technical experts of the same discipline is likely, in brainstorming, to produce an extension of the ideas along their normal lines of thinking. A group of diverse backgrounds is more likely to produce diverse ideas, a lateral approach and new insights. Such solutions arise from a recentring or a refocusing of the problem.

The candidates should have shown effective interpersonal behaviour in normal meetings. Excessively dominant or insecure people should be avoided.

A wide range of seniorities within the group will make the leader's task more difficult but may increase the chances of progressing ideas subsequently.

Pre-meeting preparation

Wherever time permits the client should be interviewed and a brief analysis of the problem obtained in terms of constraints, obstacles and objectives. The résumé of the meeting should then be circulated to participants a few days before the actual brainstorming session, together with a few notes about procedure.

Conducting a brainstorming session

Imagine we are looking at a small firm that is wanting to undertake a day's idea-generation activities as part of a drive towards developing new products. Facilities include the provision of a spacious and comfortable office, flip-charts and easel for recording ideas.

A warm-up session

Assuming that the group is inexperienced, it would probably find it difficult to achieve a high level of speculation and obey the postponement of judgement principle very rapidly. There would thus need to be a preliminary session in which to induce an atmosphere conducive to brainstorming. During such a session the principles of creativity and creativity-spurring techniques might be explained and participants might be encouraged to try out a few simple creativity tests. Towards the end of the exercises group members might be encouraged to postpone judgement during the production of ideas, again as a preparation for the subsequent brainstorming exercise.

The process of brainstorming

The exercise involves the group leader, a scribe (plus helper), the brainstormers and the client. The brainstormers' and client's roles are fairly obvious. The leader's role is to progress and pace the session – providing unobtrusive guidance where appropriate. The scribe's and helper's roles are to record the ideas generated on a flip-chart (see Figure 6.2) and to attach completed charts to the wall so that they can be easily seen by all present.

The first stage involves having the client state the problem succinctly and having him or her clarify any particular points with respect to the problem about which members are unsure. Next, a formal statement of the problem, given by the client, is recorded on the chart and this is then followed by a series of redefinitions of the problem to be offered by the

How to introduce
products that are
winners

How to introduce
winning products

Figure 6.2   Record all definitions and ideas on a flip-chart.

group. Roughly a dozen redefinitions seems to be an adequate number (though there are no hard and fast rules about this). Some of the redefinitions might split the problem as given into subproblems, some might redefine it as though looking at it in a new way, while some might adopt a metaphorical approach, for example:

☐ How to introduce new products which are winners (problem as given).

☐ How to identify winning new products (subproblem).

☐ How to satisfy customers' wants and needs (looking at the problem in a new way).

☐ How to get the horse first past the post (metaphorical approach).

In the course of problem redefinition attempts at evaluating the relative merits of the redefinitions of a complex problem can be obtained by examining it from different viewpoints. Far from conflicting with each other, they are likely to illustrate different facets of the problem situation. The client is invited to indicate those redefinitions which present the problem in a new light and which appear to be more useful than the original definition. These are then used as the starting points for the idea generation stages which follow.

Idea generation

At the ideation stage the leader selects one or more of the redefinitions of the problem nominated by the client. If more than one redefinition is selected then each one is taken in turn for ideation. Naturally, one might expect to find a completely different set of ideas generated in the case of each of the selected problem redefinitions.

The leader takes the first of the nominated problem redefinitions and the scribe writes it down on a sheet of the flip-chart. The group then begins to generate ideas which are all written up and numbered sequentially on sheets of the flip-chart. As one sheet becomes full it is posted up on the wall for all members of the group to scan. The leader may attempt to increase the tempo of idea production by asking idea-spurring questions of the following types:

☐ How can we do that?

☐ What else might do that?

☐ Can we combine that idea with any other?

This kind of approach can usually lead to the generation of 50 or more ideas in less than a quarter of an hour.

Classical brainstorming: an illustration

Problem as given:
How to improve interdepartmental relations.

Redefinitions

☐ How to be more organizationally efficient.
☐ How to get troublesome departments to cooperate.
☐ How to develop corporate sense of identity.
☐ How to create harmonious work.

Problem taken:
How to create harmonious work.

Ideation stage:

(1) Create a sense of purpose.
(2) Employ a good conductor.
(3) Wave a magic wand.
(4) Hire a good fairy.
(5) Encourage social outings – for example, to Christmas pantomimes.
(6) Develop strategic alliances between departments.
(7) Discuss how to achieve common goals.
(8) Discuss common problems.
(9) Bring in organizational consultants.
(10) Hold brainstorming sessions to generate possible ideas.
(11) Get rid of all departments and replace with one computer.
(12) Get rid of computers.
(13) Encourage human relationships, discourage mechanistic thinking.
(14) Job sharing between departments.
(15) Job enrichment or enlargement across departmental boundaries.

Note: Notice how some ideas are developed from others: (2) → (3) → (4) → (9) and (1) → (7) → (8).

Brainstorming variants

Wildest idea variant
The generation of truly novel ideas is often assisted by people bringing wild ideas into the session. The leader can ask group members to try hard

to think of wild ideas and shout them out during the course of the ideation session. If participants do so it can lead to interesting practical ideas being developed from the wild ideas that are suggested. However, it may be that the group, for one reason or another, is not able to generate wild ideas in the natural course of events. In such a case it may be necessary to suspend the normal session and introduce a second variation of brainstorming based upon the production of extremely speculative ideas (wildest idea method). This variant of brainstorming involves each member of the group imagining a dream solution to the problem which disregards the constraints of reality. Then fantasy solutions are collected and written up on the flip-chart. Then each idea is briefly treated as a concept to be brainstormed until a realistic idea is developed.

Example
Problem: developing a cooperative spirit between the company and its distributors.

Fantasy solution: sell the product to customers on behalf of the distributors.

Practical solution: second own sales and marketing staff to distributors to help sell the product to customers.

Stop and go brainstorming
The rules are the same as for classical brainstorming with the exception that the session is broken up into segments. After the rules have been stated the session leader permits the group to think and shout out ideas for 3 minutes. There is then a break of 5 minutes during which complete silence is maintained, thereby encouraging incubation to take place. Then there is another 3-minute session during which ideas are generated, 5 minutes of silence, 3 minutes more idea generating, and so on.

Round-robin brainstorming
The rules again are the same as for conventional brainstorming but instead of shouting out ideas in a spontaneous, random fashion, each member takes turns at giving whatever ideas he or she may have in his or her turn. Ideas are obtained in this fashion until the session is complete.

Buzz sessions
Buzz sessions bring together brainstorming and group competition and provide a method for using larger numbers of people than would be feasible for ordinary brainstorming. A large number of people are divided into small groups and each group has a chairperson who understands the process of brainstorming techniques. Each group brainstorms the same problem in a conventional manner and after the session each group selects

the best idea or several best ideas and the group leader presents them to the rest of the groups.

The above are only a small number of the various approaches to brainstorming that can be adopted. Techniques other than classical brainstorming represent a conscious effort to improve on the basic process.

Are brainstorming techniques useful?
The research findings with regard to the effectiveness of classical brainstorming are both numerous and contradictory. Most of the research conducted in experimental settings has produced rather negative findings while, at the same time, positive anecdotal accounts of the method have piled up (Van Gundy, 1988). The results to date are inconclusive.

Brainwriting game

Brainstorming requires a high level of leader or participant skill. A less demanding and more attractive method is provided by brainwriting (Woods, 1979) (Figure 6.3). The steps are as follows:

1. The objective of the exercise, which is to generate the most improbable idea, and a statement of the problem are first read out to the group.
2. A specified number of blank, numbered cards are bought from a facilitator. The purchaser's initials are written on a piece of paper containing numbered spaces corresponding to the card numbers.
3. The participants write down the most improbable solution they can imagine on each card they purchase.
4. The cards are then put on view for all the group participants to see.
5. Group members individually study each idea and try to convert it into a more practical idea in an attempt to reduce the individual's chances of winning. This all has to be done in silence.
6. One should allow around 20 minutes or so for the exercise. At the end of this time, each member is given two votes and told to vote – as an individual – for the two most improbable ideas. The person whose idea receives the most votes is awarded the money.
7. Two subgroups are formed and each subgroup is given half of the cards.
8. Subgroups are told to develop six practical problem solutions based on the ideas on the cards. Approximately 20 minutes should be allowed

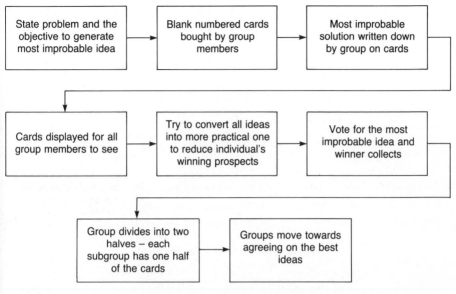

Figure 6.3 Brainwriting game.

for this purpose. Following this, each subgroup has to attempt to convince the other subgroup about the soundness of the six solutions it has developed. Finally, both subgroups then try to agree on a final list of the best ideas.

Gordon–Little variation

William Gordon, while working in association with the Arthur D. Little consulting group, produced a novel modification to classical brainstorming which is worth noting (Taylor, 1961) (Figure 6.4). He had noticed that in the course of brainstorming a problem participants often suggest what they consider to be an ideal or obvious solution and then slow down in their further creative efforts or withdraw from the brainstorming altogether. To prevent this tendency, Gordon developed a procedure that initially avoids presentation of the problem to be solved. In its place, the leader guides the group in focusing upon the underlying concept or principle of the problem. Only gradually does the leader reveal more and more information as different ideas are developed. The steps are as follows:

1. The problem is introduced in an abstract form and people are asked to think of ideas to solve the abstract problem.

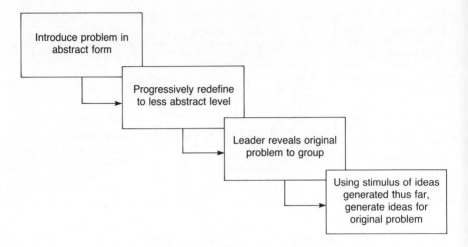

Figure 6.4   Gordon–Little variation.

2. In the course of the ideation process the leader brings in key pieces of information to do with the problem. The problem is progressively redefined to a less abstract level.
3. The leader reveals the original problem to the group.
4. Using previously generated ideas as stimuli, the group generates ideas with regard to the specific needs of the original problem.

Example
Suppose the real problem is:

How to make a warehouse layout more cost effective.

At first the problem might be defined as: how to make best use of space. Gradually, by introducing additional information, the problem would be redefined.

Story boards

Story boards have been around for centuries but were popularized by Walt Disney as a way to avoid meetings required to discuss the thousands of drawings required for animation. Advertising agencies now use story boards in their work. In the context of idea generation, Vance is usually given credit for adapting the story boards approach for idea generation (Roth, 1985) (Figure 6.5). He refers to it as the 'storybook' technique. There are also other variations on the theme produced by other people.

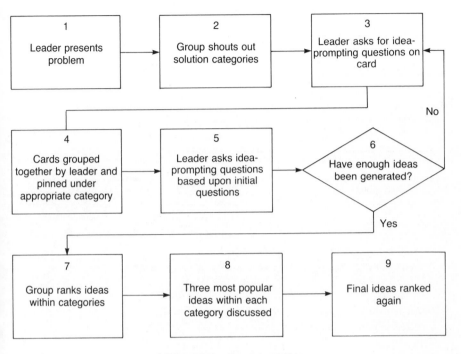

Figure 6.5 Story boards.

The storybook technique developed by Vance requires a flip-chart, corkboard, thumbtacks and several stacks of 5″ × 7″ cards. The technique proceeds as follows:

1. The problem is stated by the leader.

2. Group members indicate solution categories and each one is recorded on a card and pinned across the top of a corkboard (or some other device).

3. Idea-prompting questions are asked by the leader with respect to each category. Participants record their responses on the cards and pass them to the leader.

4. The cards are collated by the leader according to themes and he or she pins them up under the appropriate category.

5. The leader puts forward more idea-prompting questions, based upon the initial answers.

6. (3) and (4) are repeated until a sufficient number of ideas have been found.

7. The groups of ideas within the categories are ranked by the group.

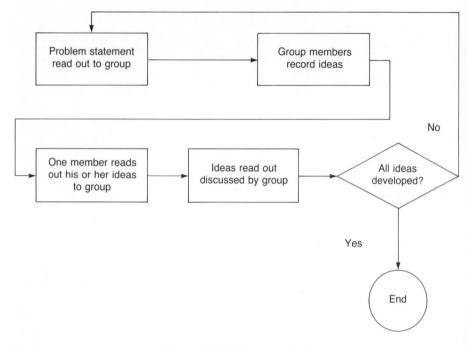

Figure 6.6 Trigger method.

8. Discussion focuses on the three most popular idea groups within each category and the leader poses idea-prompting questions.
9. Ideas are ranked again (if this is required) and implementation teams are formed.

Example
The problem may concern:

How to deal with personnel whose work is being phased out.

The first step is to generate possible idea categories, such as training, punishment, rewards and peer pressure. These are written down and pinned to the corkboard as header cards. At the next stage, the leader asks questions about the categories. For example, it might be asked how else the company might be able to make use of these employees. With the aid of such questions the participants write down their ideas on cards and pass them to the leader. These are then read out by the leader (without criticism), put into groupings by the leader and then pinned onto the board under the appropriate headings. Finally, the top three groups within each category are determined and recorded on a flip-chart. Finally, the idea groups themselves are ranked and implementation plans developed.

Trigger method

This is a method that is often used in conjunction with classical brainstorming (Bujake, 1969) (Figure 6.6). It is important when using this technique to keep to certain guidelines to ensure that it is effective. The procedure to adopt is as follows:

1. The problem statement is first read out to the group.
2. Each member of the group then has to record ideas (in silence for about 5 minutes).
3. One member of the group is then asked to read out his or her ideas to the rest of the group.
4. The ideas read out are then discussed by the rest of the group for about 10 minutes with the aim in mind to develop idea variations or even new ideas.
5. The procedure continues until all ideas have been discussed.

References

Bujake, J. E. (1969) 'Programmed innovation in new product development', *Research Management*, **12**, 279–87.

Osborn, A. (1953) *Applied Imagination*, New York: Charles Scribner and Sons.

Parnes, S. J. (1963) 'The deferment of judgement principle: a clarification of the literature', *Psychological Reports*, **12**, 521–2.

Roth, W. F. (1985) *Problem Solving for Managers*, New York: Praeger.

Taylor, J. W. (1961) *How to Create Ideas*, Englewood Cliffs, NJ: Prentice Hall.

Van Gundy, A. B. (1988) *Techniques of Structured Problem Solving*, New York: Van Nostrand Reinhold.

Woods, M. (1979) 'The brainwriting game', *Creativity Network*, **5**, 7–12.

7

Lateral thinking

Lateral thinking was originated and developed by Edward de Bono (De Bono, 1970) as a way of helping people to escape from conventional ways of looking at problems. Rather than view it as a set of creativity techniques, one should see it as a method for developing new attitudes to apply to the thinking process.

Lateral thinking is based upon the assumption that the human mind processes and stores information according to a specific pattern. However, although the storing system has a certain logic built into it, new idea development is hindered. The mind can create, recognize and use patterns but it seems unable to change them. Lateral thinking aims to disrupt the patterns by introducing discontinuity.

The introduction of discontinuity requires:

☐ an understanding of the mind's patterning system;
☐ an understanding of the difference between lateral and vertical thinking;
☐ the application of special techniques; and
☐ the use of a new operational word (see p. 124).

Vertical versus lateral thinking

Logical analysis underpins vertical thinking. Using this form of thinking we produce ideas by proceeding along a continuous logical path from one piece of information to the next. Proceeding in this way one can fairly readily determine when one has reached the objective of the exercise.

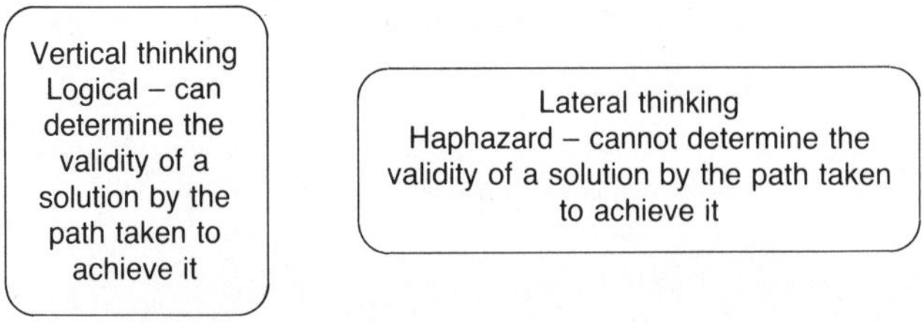

Vertical thinking
Logical – can
determine the
validity of a
solution by the
path taken to
achieve it

Lateral thinking
Haphazard – cannot determine the
validity of a solution by the path taken
to achieve it

Figure 7.1 Vertical versus lateral thinking.

By contrast, lateral thinking is a haphazard and almost illogical progression towards a solution to a problem. Moreover, even when a solution is reached one cannot determine the validity of the solution by the path taken to achieve it. In general, lateral thinking is an approach for breaking away from the mind's logical patterning to create the attitude necessary to generate new ideas. Vertical thinking, by contrast, depends upon this logical patterning to come up with specific ideas based upon the obvious (Figure 7.1).

Dimensions of lateral thinking

Three major activities go into making up lateral thinking:

☐ Awareness
☐ Alternatives
☐ Provocative methods

Awareness

The activities carried out under this heading attempt to redefine and clarify current ideas. It is argued that before old ideas can be discarded or new ones taken up, current ones must be fully understood and their limitations and good points appreciated.

De Bono suggests that current ideas can be examined from five different perspectives, as discussed below (Figure 7.2).

1. Dominant ideas
Such ideas have to be identified in order to ascertain the current perspective on the problem. In so doing it will allow subsequent generation of ideas not to be limited in scope. Different people will have different

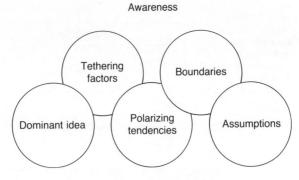

Awareness

Ideas can be examined from the above
five different perspectives

Figure 7.2 Awareness.

dominant ideas about a problem so that there may be a number of
dominant ideas. For example, during the course of a strike it may emerge
that two dominant ideas appear to exist: pay and conditions of employment. By restricting oneself to addressing only these issues one may not
reach a settlement. Some combination of resolving these dominant ideas
or issues *plus* other sweeteners may very well produce a workable
solution.

2. Tethering factors
Some factors are assumed to be included in a problem situation and are
often overlooked. For example, it is often assumed that the more we
concentrate on trying to solve a particular problem the more likely we are
to find a solution. It is possible, however, that by switching to consider
other problems we may develop insights which we can then transfer back
to the first problem. Again, one needs to identify the nature of tethering
factors that may exist in a particular situation.

A manageress was trying to figure out how to improve the management
of the cashflow during summer months when business was slack. She
concentrated on the idea for some hours but was unable to find a solution.
She then turned to deal with a pressing problem regarding a worker who
had been off sick for several months and who was in receipt of sick pay
which the firm had an obligation to pay. The idea of obligation stuck in
the mind of the manageress and on returning to the original problem she
was able to see that, by only paying bills on the date by which they had
to be settled, she could improve the cashflow situation considerably.

3. Polarizing tendencies
This kind of situation arises when the problem seems to take on the
position of an 'either–or' case. It is commonly found when only one party

to a biparty dispute can be fully satisfied. One has to try to find a solution based on compromise – possibly by redefining the problem so that neither side has to back down. When an irresistible force meets an immovable object both parties stand to lose their credibilities and their reputations!

A customer insisted that goods supplied were faulty and were not fit for the purpose for which they were intended. The store manager's first reaction was to point out that in his view the customer was, in fact, trying to use the goods for a purpose for which they were not intended and that was why the customer was experiencing dissatisfaction. However, on reflection the manager recognized that this kind of exchange of views would not resolve the situation and offered to supply the customer with something that he knew would perform the task to the customer's satisfaction – albeit at an extra cost. The customer was delighted and accepted the suggestion.

4. Boundaries

How one defines the boundaries of a problem will limit the amount of space available to solve it. It is a truism to say that many problems may exist only in the minds of those who perceive the problem. In an organizational context they may have developed from a long-existent mythology of how an organization operates and is influenced by its environment. Indeed, where a solution is proposed which ignores commonly accepted boundaries, the person presenting the solution is often accused of cheating.

Nevertheless, unless problem boundaries are considered and challenged there is a likelihood that any solutions put forward will only amount to variations on old ideas.

A commonly encountered problem is how to increase one's share of the budgetary allocation within an organization. A commonly implemented ploy is to ask for a fixed percentage more than one expects to obtain, on the assumption that the allocation given will be a given fixed percentage of whatever one seeks to obtain. Such a ploy may ensure that one's budgetary allocation does not decrease in real terms but it is unlikely that it will lead to an increase in real terms. The boundary can be extended by recognizing how people request budgetary allocations but at the same time arguing for specific allocations according to well-developed objectives, adequately supported by data, showing the benefits that will accrue from the use of the extra resource.

5. Assumptions

All ideas relating to the solution of a problem make use of assumptions. Moreover, because it is hard to check the validity of assumptions one should not try to do so, but simply acknowledge their existence. In this way new ideas may be more likely to emerge. For example, the threat of retaliatory action may be real or it may be an illusion. In advance of action

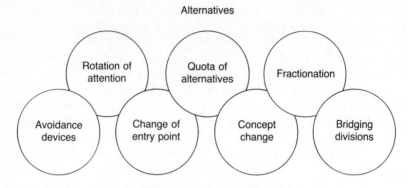

Different ways of looking at a problem

Figure 7.3 Alternatives.

it may be impossible to determine which is the case. However, if we simply recognize that retaliatory action is a possibility then the kinds of solutions we devise have to take such an eventuality into consideration.

Alternatives

This is concerned with finding as many different ways of looking at a problem as possible. It is argued that different approaches to a problem may give rise to entirely new perspectives and different ideas regarding the appropriate solution. The idea is to get away from old ideas and assumptions. There is a variety of methods which enables this to be achieved, as discussed below (see Figure 7.3).

Avoidance devices

Essentially, one has to develop an attitude of mind whereby one tends to ignore old ideas and is open to new ways of viewing a problem. Thus, for example, one should not think immediately of punitive action when a subordinate effects a misdemeanour. One should look for ways of preventing such situations from occurring and even reward people if they avoid creating such problems.

Rotation of attention

Business schools train managers to focus attention on the core of a problem. There is nothing wrong in doing this and indeed, it should certainly be encouraged. However, looking at the core of the problem may only produce familiar ideas and none of these may be deemed to provide satisfactory solutions to the problem. To get away from old ideas one may benefit from shifting to other parts of the problem. For instance, the core of a problem may seem to be how to ensure that there are adequate staffing levels to meet customer enquiries as they arise. Shifting the focus of attention to the customer and how to meet the customer's wants and needs in this instance may produce a completely different slant on the problem. For example, the problem may become how to provide a customer answer service that provides an answer to all queries within 24 hours.

Change of entry point

Analysis of a problem always has a particular starting point; the choice of starting point can exert influence and direct the search for possible solutions. In looking for new solutions the process can be greatly helped by adopting a different starting point or point of entry. First, however, one has to recognize the usual entry point and then look for a different entry point. A technique that can help is to start with a solution to the problem and then to work backwards from the solution to the starting point.

For example, a problem involved identifying how to combat new entrants to a domestic market from abroad. The first solution to the problem suggested providing higher discounts to retailers. Working back from this solution, the entry point for the problem indicated that maintaining dealer loyalty was seen as the problem. A different starting point was next considered – how to raise the barriers to entry to the market. A suggested solution was through rapid product innovation. The firm was able, subsequently, to reach an agreement to market a replacement technologically superior product under license from another firm and so stave off foreign competition.

Quota of alternatives

While the general principle in trying to generate insights is that quantity produces quality, in terms of specifying how to look at a problem it is important to identify ways that are quite distinct from one another. If there is too much overlap or similarity among the ways in which a problem is viewed this can lead to the generation of insights that are only marginally different from one another.

Viewing absenteeism as a syndrome of low morale on one hand and low level of motivation, on the other hand, may not produce sufficiently differentiated insights into the problem of absenteeism. Viewing absenteeism as a symptom of the poor quality of workers and contrasting it with a symptom of poor working conditions should, however, produce different insights.

Concept changing

The objective of concept changing is to avoid looking at a problem from a fixed point of view. If we always view a problem as one which is not of our own making, for example, then we will never recognize a situation where we may be at fault. If, on the other hand, we start off by asking ourselves whether the problem has arisen because of our own inadequacies, then, if we are sure that this is not the case, we can feel confident in looking for the source of the problem elsewhere.

Concept change can also be applied to whatever is the subject of the problem. If a manager views a trade union official as an organizational bandit then cooperation with the workforce may be difficult to obtain and working patterns may be punctuated with disputes and stoppages which benefit no one. If, on the other hand, the manager views the trade union official as a legitimate representative of the workers who has been mandated by them to negotiate on their behalf, then a more benign environment for work will be nurtured.

Fractionation
This involves dividing a problem into any arrangement of parts without regard to logical subdivisions. There is no correct way to subdivide a problem, since the objective of the exercise is to find a new way of looking at a problem. For instance, a problem of how to increase freight traffic on the railways may be divided into two parts: attractiveness to business and profitability.

Bridging divisions
Another way to produce new ways of looking at a problem is to put together two apparently unrelated concepts – the opposite to fractionation. In so doing it diverts attention from how different aspects of a problem are different to how they might be similar. In this case we would put together the attractiveness to business of the railways and profitability.

Provocative methods

De Bono (1970) envisages lateral thinking as a description of a mental process leading to new insights. For him 'the twin aspects of lateral thinking are first the provocative use of information and second the challenge to accepted concepts'. There are a number of operational techniques, discussed below (Figure 7.4).

Random stimulus
This method suggests that one should sample any rich set of random stimuli – for instance, a walk through Woolworth's, reading the dictionary, visiting the museum, etc. – and pick on some object or word that one sees.

Provocative methods

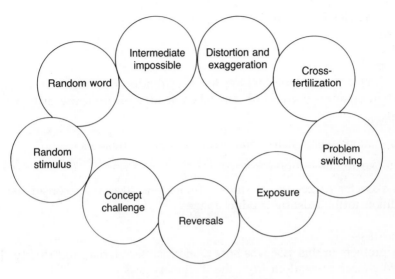

Different ways of getting ideas

Figure 7.4 Provocative methods.

The next step is to seek a relationship between the object and the problem under consideration. De Bono argues that this restructures perceptions away from preferred patterns and enriches the content of the solution set. Laennec's insight into the design of the stethoscope which stemmed from his observation of boys playing with a see-saw in an unusual way, as described in the first chapter, bears witness to the soundness of this approach.

The following provides an illustration of what is possible. A firm faced losing money unless it could find some way to reduce costs drastically. It was in the business of refurbishing cylindrical storage tanks that contained toxic chemicals. The usual process involved removing the ends of the tanks with acetylene cutting equipment, cleaning and reconditioning the surfaces both on the inside and on the outside of the tanks and then welding the component parts of the tanks back together again.

On a walk through a supermarket the fabrication manager noticed an egg slicer, which reminded him of how the slicer cut off only one end of a boiled egg thereby allowing a person to eat the whole of the contents without destroying the shell. The fabrication manager realized that the job of refurbishing the tanks could be done by removing only one end of the tank, thereby saving a considerable amount in terms of costs.

Random word

There are a number of ways in which the use of the 'random' word can be employed to aid the obtaining of new insights. Two examples are illustrated here:

Chains

The problem might be looking for new products to add to a range of kitchen equipment. A word was taken at random from the dictionary:

flower

Associations were: stalk–petals–scent–odour–air freshener–

smoke–fumes–odour–extractor

An extractor to get rid of smoke, fumes, etc. was then considered for addition to the existing product range.

Properties

The problem in this case was how to increase secretarial productivity. The word chosen at random from the dictionary was:

library

The next stage was to list the various properties of a library, and interpret their implications for secretarial staff.

☐ Holds/stores information: make optimum use of the information that secretaries acquire. Make use of them to give out and receive information.

☐ Can undertake search in order to provide information on request: secretaries are excellent researchers and can rapidly find out about much of the information held by different departments within an organization. In particular, they can discover what information is available, who has the information and how it can be accessed.

☐ Found in all cities and towns in a centrally located place: locate secretaries in part of the department or organization where they are readily visible. Visibility increases the likelihood that people will interact with them and strengthens their information-collecting role.

☐ Staffed by professionally qualified people: secretarial work should be treated as a professional occupation. A great deal of skill is required to become an efficient and effective secretary and there are internationally recognized secretarial qualifications to denote levels of competence that secretaries may have attained.

Concept challenge

Here the method involves considering in depth any important statement usually taken for granted and challenging it in all ways possible. This assists with suspension of judgement and helps one to escape from habitual thinking patterns.

Henry Ford assumed that people would be satisfied with a mass-produced standardized car. In the late 1920s his firm nearly went out of business by pursuing this business orientation. Competitors such as General Motors challenged this basic concept and differentiated the product, thereby achieving a decided competitive advantage for themselves in the market-place.

Intermediate impossible
Here we look for imaginative impossible solutions to a problem and treat them as stepping stones to more realistic solutions. For example, assume the problem is concerned with stopping pilferage by staff in a store or warehouse. The intermediate impossible would be tell staff that they can take away as much as they can carry every day, and that it is given away to them completely free. While not, perhaps, an acceptable idea in its own right it could lead to more practical solutions such as:

unlimited 'pilferage' encouraged but all staff charged a standard weekly tax calculated on the average 'pilferage' rate over a week.

A technique which is similar to the intermediate impossible, although not listed as part of lateral thinking, is wishful thinking. The basic steps of this technique are as follows:

1. The problem is stated.
2. It is assumed that anything is possible.
3. Fantasy statements such as: 'What I really need to do is . . . What really needs to happen to solve this problem is . . .' are made.
4. Each fantasy statement is examined and efforts are made to turn it into reality by making statements such as: 'Although I cannot really do that, I can . . .' or 'It might be possible to do that, but first I would have to . . .'

Rickards (1974) describes how, in looking for ways to lessen the number of deaths caused by cars impacting with lamp posts, the Road Research Laboratory 'wished' it could make a lamp post which would disappear on impact. This led eventually to the construction of a lamp post that would shear on impact, breaking and landing out of harm's way.

Reversals
The suggestion here is that one should take a problem or a threat and seek various ways of refocusing, so that the threat becomes an opportunity. This assists the *Gestalt* switch within an information field.

Distortion and exaggeration

This is a similar kind of method to that used in the case of reversals. In this case, however, it involves taking part of a situation to an extreme. The basic idea is reflected in the work of such artists as Picasso, where aspects of the human body are distorted or taken to extremes. The TV programme *Spitting Image* produces a similar effect. In practical terms for business it is perhaps best illustrated by an example. For example, assume that in selling the calls:sales ratio was found to be increasing in size. This would suggest that sales calls were, for some reason, being less successful in producing results. The situation could be exaggerated to the position where no sales calls produced sales. Under these circumstances one might think in terms of considering a totally different method of marketing altogether.

Exposure

The idea here is to 'force fit' together a stimulus which may be observed in the outside world and the problem under consideration. It is the principle of 'putting together diverse or unrelated' elements in the belief that they will enable a different insight to be gained into a problem.

For example, one might be working on the problem of how to deal with a situation where a member of staff can never be found when he or she is wanted and there is doubt as to the real authenticity of the reasons given. Walking around the park one may see the children's play area and in it a row of swings. How can features of the swings be related to the problem in hand? One may notice that all the swings are chained to a rail so that while considerable movement may be possible, the swings cannot move away from their fixed positions altogether. This may lead to considering the kinds of devices that may be used to give the individual freedom while keeping the person tethered at the same time. Communication devices such as bleepers, mobile telephones, CB radios, etc. may spring to mind.

A variation on the technique has been suggested by Geschka and Schaude and is reported in Van Gundy (1988) under the heading of Stimulus Analysis. The basic process amounts to thinking up a series of stimulus objects (unrelated to the problem), analyzing the characteristics of the objects and thence trying to produce a solution to the problem. The steps are:

1. Generate a list of 10 concrete objects.

2. Take each object in turn and break it down into its descriptive characteristics (structure, basic principles, specific ideas).

3. Each characteristic of each object is analyzed separately for stimulation possibilities and a solution is sought based upon using this stimulation.

4. The process continues until all objects and their characteristics have been studied.

5. Solutions are studied and the ones with the most potential for solving the problem are selected for further analysis.

For example, suppose the problem is how to be more effective in dealing with staff. Ten objects are selected:

Cooker	Coin
Pipe	Lamp
Sheet	Space ship
Cauliflower	Bicycle
Pen	Kennel

First, we take 'Cooker' and break it down into its characteristics: hot plates, oven, runs off electricity, made of steel, cooks food.

From this, examine:

☐ *hot plates* – suggests that one might take a tougher stance with deviant behaviour and put perpetrators on the 'hot spot';

☐ *made of steel* – suggests that a tougher, harder line should be taken when trying to get things done;

☐ *cooks food* – need to work hard on developing people in the organization and build up less superficial and more in-depth well-cooked relationships.

The process is continued for the other nine articles listed and the best ones taken for further analysis.

Cross-fertilization
In this case stimulation is provided by people. One simply takes a person who is an expert in one domain and asks them how they might deal with a problem in another. Again, it follows through the principle of putting together diverse elements.

An example might be found on a civil engineering job, where a new stretch of motorway has to built across marshland. The expert called in is an ornithologist who is well versed on how birds build their nests in marshy terrains. His suggestion is to float the motorway across the marsh on the equivalent of small man-made floating islands.

Problem switching
Exposure and cross-fertilization are combined in the method of problem switching. In principle it involves ceasing to work on one problem to move

to another, and then back to the original problem at a later stage. The theory is that new ideas may emerge from working on the new problem which can be used in the original. This is also akin to the situation of tethering factors, discussed above.

A new operational word

Po is a symbol developed by de Bono to indicate that the principles of lateral thinking should be applied. In the same way that *no* is used to reject an idea in the context of vertical thinking, the word *po* indicates that a new patterning system is to be introduced through discontinuity. *Po* is often used in conjunction with the intermediate impossible. It signifies that one should not reject or accept an intermediate idea which may seem completely unacceptable, but that judgement should be deferred for the time being.

Analogies

The use of analogies is a major topic and is developed further in the chapter on synectics. However, de Bono discusses it as a major element in lateral thinking, so we will develop the method here in the first instance.

An analogy makes a statement about how objects, people, situations or actions are similar in process or in relationship to one another. A statement such as:

'the car purrs along like a kitten'

epitomizes the analogy.

Analogies facilitate new problem perspectives, without which the solution to a problem may never be found. De Bono argues that the best analogies are those that create movement and that appear to take on a life of their own. In going about day-to-day problems it is sometimes useful, when stuck, to think of something that is similar to the problem under consideration. This often provides a new insight.

A more formal way to use analogies to generate ideas is as follows:

1. Think of other things which involve the same basic concept or actions as are involved in the subject of the problem.
2. List all the similar concepts and their associated activities.
3. Examine all the analogies and select one that looks interesting or one in which the idea generators have considerable knowledge. Elaborate on the analogies.

4. Use the descriptors generated to come up with ideas about the original problem.

For example, suppose the problem concerns how to improve time keeping in the company. The first step is to identify other things which may involve improvements:

☐ road improvement schemes
☐ cosmetic surgery
☐ developing skills

Suppose one selects road improvement schemes for the analogy. Elaboration of the analogy might produce the following:

(a) consideration of traffic flows: timing and intensity;
(b) making use of alternative routes while improvements are being carried out;
(c) imposition of speed limits during operations; and
(d) need traffic lights and cones to control disruption to traffic.

Using the descriptors as stimuli the following ideas may be generated for the original problem:

1. Staggered starting hours: staff can choose those they prefer.
2. Putting some people into jobs that required starting times which they can more easily work to.
3. Different working days dependent upon efficiency of getting the job done – for example, do 5 days' work in 4 days and only attend for 4 days but be paid for 5 days.
4. Markers to show how well or how badly people are 'time keeping'.

Another example is given in the case of the woman manager who is trying to develop a team of young people in a work situation. Trying to think up ideas is not always that easy, but here analogies can help. It was suggested to the manager that she took the analogy of making a cake and that she wrote down the various stages and elements that went into baking a cake. She wrote down the following list:

☐ obtain the ingredients;
☐ collect together the kitchen utensils;
☐ measure out the ingredients;

- start to preheat the oven to the correct temperature;
- mix the ingredients in a bowl;
- put the mixture on a well-greased tray;
- put the tray into the oven at predetermined temperature;
- cook for a certain length of time;
- check periodically by 'pricking' the cake to see how it is baking; and
- remove from the oven when cooked and allow to cool.

The next stage involves working through the items in the list and seeing how these can be directly translated into the situation of developing the young people in the office. In this case there are several interpretations, depending on the particular stance taken. One such interpretation might be:

- select the young people carefully;
- assemble all the training–developmental aids;
- determine what each person requires in the way of training and development;
- set in motion the training programme;
- prepare the people for training and development;
- equip them with the right kind of expectations;
- send them on to the training programme when the time is right;
- provide the correct amount of training for each individual;
- obtain feedback of information from time to time to ensure that the right kind of progress is being made; and
- let them have time to settle into their jobs after training and development has taken place.

References

De Bono, E. (1970) *Lateral Thinking: Creativity step by step*, New York: Harper & Row.
Rickards, T. (1974) *Problem Solving Through Creative Analysis*, Aldershot: Gower.
Van Gundy, A. B. (1988) *Techniques of Structured Problem Solving*, New York: Van Nostrand Reinhold.

8

Synectics and related approaches

Synectics is the name given to a body of knowledge, a collection of behavioural skills and a set of problem-solving techniques. It is also the international group of companies that have developed this from 30 years of study and work with innovative groups. In this chapter we look first at metaphors in general before proceeding to examine the case for synectics.

Metaphors

When one applies a figure of speech to something to which it is not literally applicable, then this is referred to as a metaphor. To say that one has 'nerves of steel' is an example of a metaphor. Metaphors are very similar to analogies and can be used to create a fantasy situation for gaining new problem perspectives.

In making use of metaphors in creative problem solving one proceeds as follows:

1. State the problem.
2. Select a metaphor.
3. Use the metaphor to generate new ideas.

Example
Imagine one is trying to improve communications within an organization. The metaphor of a 'journey' might be examined as a possible means of gaining new insights. Journeys often have bottlenecks at which traffic is

127

clogged up and delays and frustrations occur. The metaphor may lead one to looking at ways of speeding up the flow of information, reducing communication bottlenecks and breaking up information into manageable chunks.

Beth Rogers (1993) provides a good discourse on and an excellent example of the use of the metaphor. She argues that the purpose of using analogy and metaphor is to raise sensitivity to a level which enables long-term common sense to prevail. Domestic situations are ideal – such as comparing cash flow to a plumbing system, and staff development to gardening. When it comes to strategy, history is the very best starting point. She suggests that if, by application of imagination, companies can avoid the type of mistakes made by Charles I or Napoleon, the exercise has to be worthwhile.

Beth Rogers used the fairly common comparison of marketing campaigns with military campaigns in a workshop with a team responsible for a product which was in slow decline, while its successors were still in the laboratories. The company was facing a few difficult years of transition. She presented the analogy of medieval siege warfare, which helped the attenders to work out strategies to defend the declining product.

The group identified the need for developing 'solidarity' with existing customers and providing reassurance. They also identified the risks associated with launching the new products. Market research was required, and alliances with third parties who influence buying decisions. After all, the commander of a besieged city would not counter-attack without the very best intelligence about where to target his forces, and expectations of help from allies.

Synectics

Synectics was originally developed by William Gordon, who observed individual problem-solving activity and inferred from it the psychological processes involved. Gordon was later joined by George Prince at Arthur D. Little and together they established Synectics Incorporated in Cambridge, MA, United States. In 1960. Gordon left the company and both men established their own versions of synectics. The main difference in the two approaches is in the terminology of the two approaches.

Literally, the word 'synectics', stemming from the Greek, means the fitting together of disparate elements. Throughout his writings, Gordon emphasized the need to 'make the familiar strange' in order to increase the possibility of gaining new insights into problems. Synectics is a process for a group of individuals working on a problem in an oddball manner.

The approach emphasizes the nonrational substance of thought in the expectation that such a method will give an original and certainly a stimulating slant to a problem.

Synectics uses analogies and metaphors to both analyze a problem and develop possible solutions. The use of analogies and metaphors encourages use of material which on first sight may seem altogether inapplicable to a problem. Two operational mechanisms are used. The first is making the strange seem familiar and is designed to allow the user a better understanding of the problem by viewing it in a new way. The second is making the familiar strange and this attempts to pull the problem solver away from the problem so that a more creative solution can be found.

The purpose of these mechanisms is to produce five psychological states that are necessary to achieve creative responses:

- □ involvement and detachment;
- □ deferment;
- □ speculation;
- □ autonomy of object; and
- □ hedonic response.

It is argued that only when these states are reached that the unconscious and irrational aspects of the mind can be merged with the conscious and rational to attain greater creative efficiency.

Nature of the psychological states

Involvement and detachment

When involvement is experienced there is a feeling of being tied to a problem to such an extent that it cannot be avoided. There is a definite feeling of wanting to understand a problem. Detachment is the opposite – the feeling that one is on the outside and looking in. Both are necessary for the development of creative solutions.

Deferment

This is the avoidance of premature solutions. A danger exists in applying the obvious and immediately available solution, since better solutions may be overlooked. Immediate solutions should be temporarily set aside.

Speculation

The capacity of the members of a group to allow their minds to run free. Development of such an attitude indicates receptiveness to considering the impossible or nearly impossible.

Autonomy of object

As a problem solver moves closer to the final solution, a feeling develops that the problem is 'outside' the problem solver. The problem seems to appear as if it has an identity of its own and is no longer in the control of the problem solver. This needs to be encouraged.

Hedonic response

This is a feeling of being on the right track without having any validating evidence to support it.

Membership of a synectics group

The effective use of the techniques also require close attention being given to the problem-solving process and the roles that the participants play in using the method. It is a relatively structured approach and a trained leader is required for guiding the group through the different stages and for integrating the comments of the original problem poser. Unless the problem-solving activity is carefully orchestrated, the required psychological states are not likely to be attained and a good quality solution is unlikely to emerge.

Gordon laid down quite specific criteria for group membership and composition. He suggested that group members should be frequent users of analogies and metaphors; have an attitude of assistance, well coordinated bodily movements and the capacity to generalize. They should possess personality traits such as emotional maturity, 'constructive childishness' and 'risk taking' and be non-status orientated. They needed to show a commitment to the group and its purpose and be 25–40 years of age.

The group should not have too many experts. The problem owner will invariably be the problem content expert. It is easier on the leader if all are of equal status and it is useful to have a couple of people who are good at coming up with wild ideas. These people may set the cultural norm of the group which otherwise might be unwilling to try wild ideas. It is also advantageous to have some members who have been trained in the use of synectics.

The problem owner

He or she should be warned of what to expect, so that he or she is not alarmed when the proceedings appear to be running off in a seemingly irrelevant direction. It is also useful for the problem owner to understand the synectics process.

He or she must have the authority and resources to implement a solution when one is found. He or she should also be encouraged to explore beyond the problem as originally stated, to see if there may not be more appropriate ways of looking at the problem – particularly if the problem stated is of a general nature.

The group leader

The role is that of a process leader who guides only the problem-solving process. The leader should not become involved with the problem content in any way. Leaders should direct the process, not contribute ideas, suggestions or possible solutions, let alone the best way of resolving the problem. The group leader should determine the success of the process by observing, and asking for, the client's reactions to what is going on.

The synectics session leader needs to be seen as serving the needs of the group in order to gain commitment, enthusiasm and the best ideas. The group leader is also responsible for:

☐ ensuring that the group members obey the rules;

☐ encouraging speculation;

☐ logging all the ideas;

☐ checking with the problem owner that the group is on the right track; and

☐ managing the time.

He or she needs to be trained. Some desirable characteristics of good synectics group leadership are shown in Figure 8.1.

A good synectics group leader should

(a) never go into competition with the group
(b) be a good listener to team members
(c) not allow anyone to be put on the defensive
(d) keep the energy level high
(e) use every member of the team
(f) not manipulate the team

Figure 8.1   Characteristics of good synectics group leadership.

The group

Since the group may generate ideas faster than the leader can write them down on the flip-charts, group members should be encouraged to jot ideas down on notepads until required. Half-formed and wild ideas should be recorded. Group members should support each other's efforts by complimenting them where appropriate.

Features of synectics

No attempt is made to define the problem. The client's statement of the problem is taken as the starting point; he or she gives a brief explanation of the background, as he or she sees it, and the group and client proceed to restate or paraphrase the problem in a language of 'How to' statements. These can be as speculative, unrealistic, wishful or challenging as the group feels inclined to produce. Their purpose is to open up the whole problem area and give the client an opportunity to get away from his or her conventional way of looking at the problem.

'Stay loose 'till rigour counts'.

This synectics slogan expresses a basic feature of the process. Rigour, precision, accuracy, realism are necessary and valuable in their place, but they are not the stuff of which creativity is made. We have to make a conscious effort to suspend normal acceptable intellectual standards if we are to give free rein to speculation, imagination and originality.

Conventional treatment of ideas makes two assumptions about the nature of ideas: first, they are monolithic entities and secondly, their value is binary – good or bad. Our experience is that both these assumptions are incorrect and destructive. An idea is not monolithic, it has many facets. There is always something good about an idea.

As with brainstorming the group leader is a facilitator–recorder of data and does not play any other active role in the proceedings. The other members of the group may number from five to ten and comprise people who may or may not have competent expertise in the subject matter to be considered.

Operational mechanisms

Synectics employs a number of mechanisms for making the familiar strange:

☐ Personal analogy.

☐ Direct analogy.

☐ Symbolic analogy.

☐ Fantasy analogy.

Personal analogy

All of us possess emotions and feelings. This mechanism harnesses the use of our emotions and feelings in order to obtain insights into problems which are purely technological in nature. The idea is to identify oneself with a non-human object which is the subject of the problem. One has to transfer one's own feelings into the entity and imagine how it might feel and act in the problem situation.

An individual has to imagine that he or she is actually the object under study. One might be asked to imagine what it feels like to be that particular object in a given situation. There are at least four possible degrees of involvement:

1. Describing the object by listing its basic characteristics.
2. Describing the emotions the object might have in a given situation – for example, how tired a door hinge might become from opening and shutting.
3. How a person feels when using the object.
4. Describing what it feels like to be the given object (as at beginning above).

Example
One might be asked to imagine what it would feel like to be a new model of a popular make of car. Based upon such an analysis it might then be

possible to develop advertising themes to aim at specific customer groups. The reader might like to try to verbalize his or her feelings about this. It is through such a technique that we are able to release ourselves from looking at a problem in terms of its previously analyzed elements.

Direct analogy

This is a mechanism by which we try to make comparisons with analogous facts, information or technology. In making use of this device we have to search our experiences and knowledge to collect together phenomena that seem to exhibit relationships familiar with those of the problem in hand.

It should be borne in mind, however, that if the relationships we consider are too close to the problem in hand then we will not make the familiar strange and it is less likely that we will gain any useful insights. If, for example, we were to compare a motor car with a bicycle then this could be too close a parallel to evoke useful insights. The comparison of a computer with the human brain, on the other hand, could be useful. Indeed, it is often fruitful to compare animate systems with inanimate systems or to make comparisons between biological, ecological and other natural science systems and social systems. Attributes of atoms and molecules, for example, provide interesting analogies for studying the management of information.

This is perhaps the most basic and most valuable kind of analogy. The idea is to try to describe a clear and straightforward relationship between the problem and some object, thing or idea. One could compare the opening and closing of a door hinge to a similar feature of a clam shell. Biological organisms are a rich source of direct analogies.

Example
Suppose the problem concerns finding the best way of dealing with routine information flow in and out of the office. In using an analogy we can look at how people deal with the problems created by the flow of water in a large river. At times, very little water may flow down the river and under such circumstances the river creates problems for people if they depend upon it for irrigation, navigation or some other use. A similar position occurs in the office, since a continual flow of information is required to enable smooth running of the office.

Similarly, a large river may sometimes be in flood after heavy rains or when snow melts high in the mountains, causing tributaries to increase the volume of water they feed into the mainstream of the river. Too great a flow of water can cause flooding and damage to land and towns close to the course of the river. By analogy too much information also creates problems. There may be insufficient office workers to deal with it, or it may be overly complex and difficult to analyze.

In both these cases we have to look at how people deal with the problems that too little and too much water in the river can cause. For example, one can create several reservoirs on a river and thereby control the amount of water flowing in the river throughout the year. By analogy, we could perhaps create reservoirs of information with the added feature of having specific deadlines by which we deal with or pass on information. Similar time limits might also be imposed by which we expect to receive certain information. In other words, we need to set up procedures and a filing system to control both the inflow and the outflow of information through the office.

Symbolic analogy

According to Gordon, this analogy makes use of objective and personal images to describe a problem. Gordon (1961) describes a problem of how to design a jacking mechanism that will fit into a 4″ × 4″ box and yet extend 3′ upwards and support 4 tons. In the course of group discussion of the problem one of the members suggested that the problem is 'like an Indian rope trick'. Using this suggestion as a stimulus (once the familiar had been made strange) the group then proceeded to develop a practical application of the Indian rope trick and solved the problem. (The problem was solved by adopting the mechanics of a bicycle chain, which unfolds in one direction. The linking together of two chain-like mechanisms creates a jack that is both flexible and strong enough to support a heavy object.)

Fantasy analogy

This is based on Freud's notion that creative thinking and wish fulfilment are strongly related. An artist, for example, has certain creative needs that are satisfied only by wishing for something that is eventually translated into a work of art. Synectics both borrows this idea and operationalizes it. One group used it to develop a vapour-proof suit for space suits. This involved a rubber and steel spring mechanism that solved the problem, and this was accomplished by asking the question:

How do we in our wildest fantasy desire the closure to operate?

Example
Suppose we are experiencing increasing costs and that none of our competitors are increasing their prices. We are trying to find a way of

keeping our product as competitive in the market-place as others' products. Using a fantasy analogy we might pose the question:

How do we in our wildest fantasy increase the price of the product without seeming to increase the price?

This may lead eventually to such ideas as:

1. The discount structure can be altered so that the total profit to the company is increased but the list price to customers remains the same.
2. The minimum order size is increased so that small orders are eliminated and overall costs thereby reduced.
3. Delivery and special services are charged for.
4. Invoices are raised for repairs on purchased equipment.
5. Charge for engineering, installation and supervision.
6. Customers are made to pay for overtime required to send out urgent orders.
7. Interest is collected on overdue accounts.
8. Lower margin models in the product line are eliminated and more profitable ones sold in their place.
9. Escalator clauses are built into bids for contracts.
10. The physical characteristics of the product are changed – for instance, it is made smaller.

Synectics process

In synectics a flow chart gives a step by step outline of what the group should do. Many variations and options are open to the leader. The flow chart described below represents the simplest 'excursion' available (see also Figure 8.2). Typically, meetings are held in a room equipped with several large newsprint easel pads.

Stages of the synectics process

There are eight stages, as follows:

1. Problem as given
A general statement of the problem is read to the group.

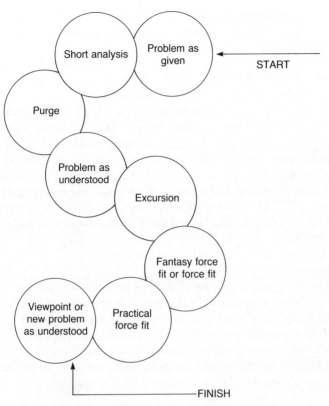

Figure 8.2 Stages of the synectics process.

2. Short analysis of the problem as given
The main purpose of this stage is to make the strange familiar. This can be achieved in a number of ways: for example, the group can make use of metaphors and analogies.

3. Purge
Eliminate the rigid and superficial solution suggested in the first two stages. This also helps to clarify the problem statement. The next step is called the 'Purge'. When people hear of a problem they think of solutions. This is an opportunity to suggest them. These are referred by the group to the expert for evaluation. Quite often it is something the expert has tried; he explains what happened and why it did not work. Sometimes the solution will be new and promising to the expert. This is written on a sheet of newsprint labelled 'Viewpoints'.

4. Problem as understood

This stage begins with a selection of a part of a problem to work on. To do this each participant describes how he or she sees the problem using, if possible, a fantasy analogy or wishful thinking. The leader then writes down each of the viewpoints. One is chosen, in conjunction with the expert or problem owner for further analysis.

Each person in the group privately writes one or more versions of the problem as he or she sees it. Alternatively, or in addition, each member of the group is encouraged to state as a problem wishful, ideal versions, for instance 'how can we make the fabric turn . . . if it is weak'. The temporary leader writes all 'the problems as understood' on the newsprint pads and uses them for subsequent 'excursions'. He or she then chooses the one he or she wants to work with, tells the group, and requests that they put the whole problem out of their conscious minds and simply do as he or she says.

5. Excursion

This part of the process may be viewed as an artificial vacation or holiday from the problem. It is during this stage that operational mechanisms are used. The leader asks questions that will require or evoke an analogical answer. Following the generation of a number of analogies, the leader might then select one for detailed analysis and elaboration. Typically the leader will select an analogy on the basis of its irrelevance to the problem and the group's knowledge and interest in the analogy.

6. Fantasy force fit or force fit

Here we find a divergence between the approaches proposed by Gordon and by Prince. Gordon's approach is to force a fit between the last analogy used in the excursion stage and the problem as understood. In Gordon's case, the use of fantasy during this stage helps to produce more creative responses. In contrast, Prince takes a somewhat more structured approach to develop a force fit. One of his methods is to use a 'forced metaphor' in which the group considers the two elements to be forced and tries to make a connection by speculating wildly. Whatever way is adopted the group has to work with the problem and the analogies until a new way of looking at the problem is found.

7. Practical force fit

At this stage a practical application of the analogy developed at the previous stage is made. For example, in trying to find ways of attracting more customers, the analogy of the Trojan Horse may be first used to develop a fantasy force fit. In this case the analogy involves providing something that customers will want so much that they will be unable to resist the temptation to purchase. The next step is to remove the fantasy force fit and develop more practical applications. One answer is to give away free samples.

8. Viewpoint or new problem as understood

The synectics process has to end with the production of a viewpoint (a new way of looking at the problem). Once a viewpoint is selected expert guidance needs to be provided to transform the viewpoint into a solution to the problem.

One should work through about eight stages, although not sticking rigidly to a prescribed format. There are three major parts:

☐ defining and analyzing the problem;

☐ increasing understanding or making the familiar strange; using operational mechanisms to make the familiar strange; and

☐ integrating (or force fitting) the results of using the operational mechanisms with the problem.

Example

The format adopted in this illustration is as follows:

1. State the problem/goal wish.
2. Take a key word from the statement and ask for examples in a different domain – for example, nature.
3. Take an example generated from (2) above and ask what it feels like to be that example.
4. Pick one of the feelings generated – for example, to be permanent and ask what might be needed to change that state.
5. Take ideas generated in (4) above and see how they can be related back to the problem.

A group was attempting to solve a problem of people not getting on with their assigned jobs in an office. Work was not progressing smoothly through the office and jobs were delayed or sometimes not done at all. Previously, several convergent approaches had been tried, with limited success.

The group leader decided to use an excursion as a way of taking the group away from the problem. It had been with them for several weeks and the leader felt that they were simply too close to it – too locked into ideas already known to them.

The problem was defined as 'how to improve the throughput of jobs through an office'. This was subsequently redefined to 'how to remove the flaws in the office organization'.

The leader took a key word from the problem definition – flaws. The group were then asked to offer any thoughts about flaws from the world of nature, choosing nature because of its distance from the office. Ideas generated included rift valleys, scars on the landscape, hybrid creatures and monsters, and cancerous growths.

Again, to create a distance between the problem and the group, the leader asked what it felt like to be a scar on the landscape. Some responses were: ugly, unwanted, unnecessary and a natural thing.

The leader then followed on the 'natural thing' issue (seeing its possible relation to the problem) and asked the group what would be necessary to make *you* feel *not* a natural thing when *you* are a scar on the landscape. Replies included:

☐ Show the damage you cause to the environment.

☐ Point out how out of keeping you are with your surroundings.

☐ Show you what a natural scar on the landscape really is and how it can, in fact, be quite attractive.

The leader next asked the group to associate these ideas with the original problem: the 'showing damage to the environment' seemed immediately relevant. This was interpreted to mean understanding the negative effects on overall company performance that the inefficiencies in the office could create – lost sales and profits, increased costs, etc. Devising some kind of monitoring device which would show the impact of these inefficiencies was considered to be the next step.

Eventually, a system was developed which measured the impact of major deficiencies or errors in the office and the impact they had on sales, profits and costs.

General observations

Some other general comments are as follows:

1. The problem owner should not be allowed to describe every intricate detail of the problem situation.
2. At the 'goal orientation' stage one should try to view the problem situation in a variety of ways, so that one looks for a solution in the most appropriate direction. 'Goal wishing' stresses that speculation–wishing is permitted and desired. We are seeking different angles or redefinitions of the problem. This is a time when the group members must not evaluate their own ideas. Way-out ideas often trigger other ideas in group members. The problem owner should offer directions

as to which of the ideas appear to offer the best way forward and so direct the group members. 'How to' or 'I wish' statements are quite useful. The latter encourages speculation, while the former conveys positive direction.

Selection

The problem owner needs a chance to reflect on the redefinitions generated and select two or three that best describe the problem situation. He or she should be warned against selecting only those that appear obviously practical, and be advised to choose those that are intriguing, novel and interesting. The problem owner is asked to say what led him or her to choose the selected 'springboards'.

If no specific action is indicated by a 'springboard', the next step is to generate ideas as to how the circumstances it describes might be brought about; possibly by using an excursion.

Excursion

Various types of excursion are used in the synectics process. The choice of excursion depends on the degree of novelty required in a solution, the element of risk the leader is prepared to take and the type of material that is being worked upon. Hicks (1991) distinguishes between 'imaging or fantasy excursion' and 'example excursion'. The imaging excursion is possibly the most unorthodox form of excursion and can be a potential disaster with a conservative-minded group – although it often works dramatically well when it is least expected and produces the most innovative ideas.

For a fantasy or image excursion the group is asked to describe a mental picture/story inspired by the last item in a word association preliminary exercise, starting with a word taken from the 'springboard'. One person will lead off and then every other person in the group has to add to the story. They should be invited to jump in whenever they like and be told that the more colourful, outlandish, weird or exotic the story the better. It is usually better to keep the story in the same location, if possible, as this makes for better imagery. Everyone should try to add about a minute to the story and then someone else takes over. The changeover may be left to the discretion of the leader.

If the story tends to stagnate on some minute detail of one particular image the leader can ask someone to make something surprising happen. Conversely, if images are insufficiently developed because story-tellers move too quickly to other images the leader can pin people to one scenario by asking for more detail. People may be anxious about producing mental images in public and about ability to contribute to the story. It is, however, the violent changing of direction and having to build another mental image after the destruction of the first that makes the story rich in speculation and evocative images.

Absurd solutions

When every group member has had at least one chance to contribute to the story the leader stops the imaging and asks the group to replay the story in their minds and try to think up some really absurd or impractical solutions to the problem. The absurd solutions are written on the flip-chart.

Having moved so far from the problem with the fantasy excursion it usually becomes desirable to return to the real world and the problem in several stages, the first of which is this drawing-up of absurd solutions. If a group member immediately comes up with a sensible and novel solution one should obviously not reject it.

The leader needs to check with the problem owner to see if any of the absurd solutions intrigue, fascinate or appeal to them. There should be no problem with picking too practical a solution as there should not be any. After the problem owner makes his or her selection the leader asks the group to examine the chosen absurd solutions and to try to find ways of changing them into something more practical and closer to reality, while retaining as much of the original idea as possible. It is better not to attempt to do this in one step but to spend some time modifying them, because there is a tendency to lose the novel feature contained in the absurd solution by jumping back to reality too quickly.

Itemized response (IR)

We should not reject ideas which are not perfectly formed. Indeed, the suggestion is to work on and develop the ideas into more practical solutions. Synectics has developed a simple technique, itemized response (IR), that allows a possible solution to be developed from any idea, using gentle evaluation that encourages the ironing-out of minor concerns rather than dismissal of the idea. It starts from the assumption that all ideas have value, and thus before any flaws or imperfections in the idea are pointed out, first some of the good points (perhaps three to five) are listed. This reinforces the value of the idea, and justifies the additional time that will be spent overcoming concerns about it.

The problem owner is asked to identify practical, helpful or attractive aspects of an idea, giving reasons wherever possible. It may be helpful to let the group also contribute to this, since they may see benefits not immediately apparent to the problem owner. The leader asks for the problem owner's major concern with the idea, expressing this as a 'how to/I wish' to give the group a direction for further development of the idea, in order to overcome this concern. The leader then gathers ideas from the group and writes them on the flip-chart while asking the problem owner to paraphrase the suggestions to ensure understanding. If the group comes up with a suggestion that only partially overcomes the concern the IR process is repeated with this latest suggestion. As the idea develops in this way it becomes more difficult to get three 'new' good points each time, but the time spent trying is usually worthwhile.

Having resolved the major concern, the group tackles other concerns the problem owner may have with respect to the original idea, always taking them one at a time. The process continues, gradually homing in on a possible solution, a course of action which the problem owner can implement without further help from the group. The leader then writes up the possible solution.

When to use synectics, and its limitations

Synectics is an ideal strategy to adopt if innovation is sought, or a particularly novel solution is desired, but this should not be seen as a limiting factor. The only real limitation on the application of synectics concerns group size. If the problem situation has more than a handful of problem owners, it will not be possible to resolve it with them as one group. A group of six to eight people seems ideal.

References

Gordon, W. J. (1956) 'Operational approaches to creativity', *Harvard Business Review*, **34**, 41–51.

Gordon, W. J. (1961) *Synectics*, New York: Harper & Row.

Hicks, M. J. (1991) *Problem Solving in Business and Management*, London: Chapman & Hall.

Rogers, E. (1993) 'Giving creativity a shot in the arm', *Involvement and Participation*, Summer, 6–10.

9

Miscellaneous idea-generating methods

A selection of other methods are presented in this chapter, including such techniques as: mind mapping, value analysis, visual metaphor, force field analysis, rich diagrams, attribute analogy chains, bionics, story writing and the Crawford slip method. In addition, scenario writing and scenario day-dreaming, along with the cross-impact matrix, are also covered. There are, of course, a long list of miscellaneous techniques but these represent a selection from among the best known.

Visual metaphor

The idea behind the visual metaphor (Majaro, 1991) is to have people represent a problem and how they see the problem solved in a pictorial form (Figure 9.1). Drawing skill is unimportant and has no bearing on the use of the technique. The steps involved are as follows:

1. People participating in the exercise draw a picture of what they consider to be the problem with which they are concerned. Words should be avoided when drawing the picture.

2. A picture of the solution to the problem is next drawn. The instruction is to simply portray the situation as it would appear if the problem had been solved.

3. People are then asked to note individually how their solution picture differs from the problem picture. Once all the changes are noted each person has then to interpret these into analogous steps which could be taken to solve the problem in real life. They have to do this without conferring.

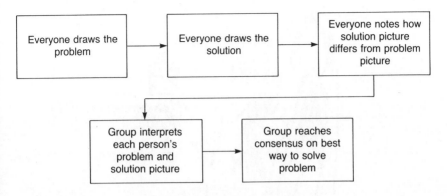

Figure 9.1 Visual metaphor.

4. The group is then asked to interpret each person's problem and solution picture.

5. In the last stage of the exercise the group discusses and collates each person's suggested steps for reaching a solution to the problem. There are usually two or three definite measures that can be taken.

Example
S supervises an office in which there are a number of junior workers and a senior assistant, V. J is S's supervisor and occupies a management position.

In the first picture (Figure 9.2), S is the figure with ringlets (top centre) and is heavily influenced by a petulant J (the figure on the left of the picture). J also has an enormous influence on the workers (the very small figures). S is not able to have a great deal of autonomy managing the situation. V is also in the picture (on the right) and J has an undesirable influence on her as well.

In the second picture (Figure 9.3), the solution is that S manages to extract herself from the influence of J, and that J and V can both influence the running of the office with S having the major influence in running it.

In the second picture (Figure 9.3), the essential difference is that J is distanced from the office workers and both S and V. This was interpreted to mean some form of physical separation or distancing or, alternatively, some form of reorganization whereby J would occupy a different role in the organization and would not be concerned in the direct supervision of S.

Visual metaphors can be used by both individuals and groups. In the former case, however, there will be a lack of stimulus to creativity that a group can provide.

Figure 9.2 The problem.

Figure 9.3 The solution.

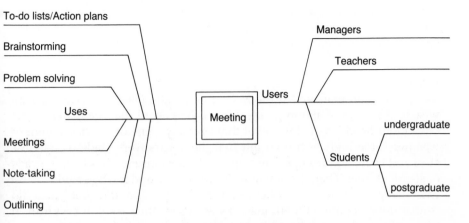

Figure 9.4 Mind-mapping, drawn using InfoMap Lite (see p. 215).

Mind-mapping

The simplest of techniques can often be the most productive. Goman (1989) notes that visual aids in various forms can be used to boost creativity. She describes a form of 'visual thinking' called 'mind-mapping' (Figure 9.4). One starts by taking a central theme and writing or drawing it in the centre of a sheet of paper. The main theme is then circled and lines drawn (like spokes) whenever new ideas come to mind, writing each idea just above the line that has just been drawn. If a particular idea suggests another association, a branch is drawn off from that line and the new idea written in.

In the illustration in Figure 9.4 we look at possible applications and users of mind-mapping as a technique and display them in the form of a mind-map.

Value analysis

Value analysis is an important aspect of product management, concerned with finding the most economical and cost-effective method of producing a product or service. In effect, the specifications of a product or service are considered in minute detail and management looks for more cost-effective ways of performing the same function. For example, a piece of equipment may be made up of all-metal parts that are relatively expensive to produce. Substitution of parts made from other materials may lower the cost of producing the equipment but without impairing performance, including its reliability. When properly carried out value engineering should prevent over- or under-engineering from occurring.

Example
The production manager of the Miles Engine and Gear Company, a man wise in the ways of spotting out-of-line costs, noted that the material cost of cylinder head inserts for one of the company's line of V8 diesel engines was much too high. It turned out that the inserts were made of stainless steel and even, according to the company's metallurgist, the cheaper grade of stainless steel. Then the metallurgist began to wonder why stainless steel was being used at all. Other engines in the line did not, nor did competitors' engines. Where inserts were used, they were of cast iron. It was a case of the seventh soldier standing to attention (because years ago he had held the mule reins) while the artillery was fired; the reason for stainless steel inserts was lost in history. The result was that the production manager ordered some inserts to be cast from valve-guide material, an inexpensive grade of iron. When several hundred engines were tested with the experimental inserts over a period of a year, no difference in performance could be detected. The changeover saved $200 per day in materials cost, based on the production rate at the time the problem was noted (from Marquis, 1969).

Force field analysis

Force field analysis facilitates the graphic representation of a problem in terms that are readily understandable and that can lead to the production of good solutions (see Majaro, 1991) (Figure 9.5). In any situation where a problem exists, it is argued, there are forces working in favour of a solution which can be harnessed to good effect in producing a solution. These forces are known as 'driving forces' and the solution strategy idea is to make it easier for these forces to work. At the same time, there are various forces that work against the implementation of a solution to a problem, known as 'restraining forces'. The idea is to lessen the impact that these forces have over a situation and the problem it contains.

Driving and restraining forces are first identified and then ranked for their degree of importance in relationship to the problem under analysis. Priority has to be given to altering the impact of high priority forces on a problem.

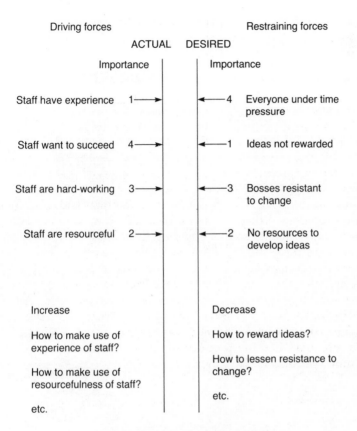

Figure 9.5 Force field analysis.

Symbolic representations

This technique uses abstract symbols related to a problem to generate ideas (see, for instance, Van Gundy, 1988). One could develop a set of symbols (see Hicks, 1991) or they can be generated intuitively at the time the technique is used (Figure 9.6). While the latter has the advantage of flexibility the former brings in the element of consistency and makes it easier for all members to appreciate the meaning of the symbols. The steps are as follows:

1. A statement of the problem is written down.
2. The problem is redefined or restated in terms of the basic underlying principle involved.
3. An abstract symbol that generally represents the principle is drawn.

Figure 9.6 Symbolic representation.

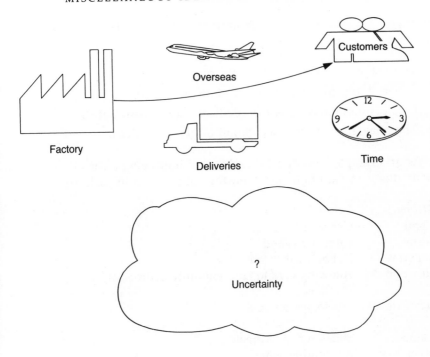

Figure 9.7 A problem in symbols.

4. This symbol is used as a starting point, and through free association another symbol, prompted by the first one, is drawn.
5. A third symbol suggested by the second one is drawn and matters proceed in this fashion, using free association, until four or five symbols have been drawn. Each symbol is used as a stimulus and any idea or ideas that it may suggest are recorded.

Example
In Figure 9.7 we see a situation stated in symbols. There is uncertainty over whether a factory can make deliveries to overseas customers on time.

Attribute analogy chains

This is a combination of attribute listing (see Chapter 5 on morphological analysis) and analogies (see Chapter 7 on lateral thinking). Attribute analogy chains (Koberg and Bagnall, 1976) generate ideas by developing analogies for each of the major problem attributes. The procedure is as follows:

1. The major problem attributes are recorded.
2. Subattributes for each major attribute are listed.
3. One or more analogy is recorded for each subattribute.
4. The analogies are used as stimuli to generate ideas.

As an example consider the problem of improving a car tyre. First we write down the attribute and then the subattribute in each case:

Attributes	Subattributes
Name	Car tyre
Form	Circular, round
Material	Rubber; steel; fabric
Function	Allowing cars to run smoothly on roads

Next, develop analogies for each attribute:

Name	Shoes for the wheels
Form	A spinning wheel
Material	Sponge; cushion of air
Function	Weighing down tarpaulins of farmers' hayricks

Ideas generated based on analogies:

1. Monitor on dashboard showing amount of tyre wear on each wheel.
2. Multicoloured tyres.
3. Semi-solid tyres: half air, half sponge/thick rubber.
4. Convertible tyres for different kinds of weather.

Bionics

This is a very specific application of analogies (see Gordon, 1961). It involves looking for idea stimulation in similar objects, products and processes. The search is, however, restricted to biological and botanical systems using the argument that Nature provides clues with regard to how to solve problems because it has itself solved many such problems.

A good example of its use is provided by the temperature-sensing organs of a rattlesnake, which sparked off the idea of the Sidewinder heat-seeking missile. Another example is Velcro, which is mentioned earlier in the book.

Nature does not always provide the right kind of guidance, however. Prior to the invention of the aeroplane many fruitless years were spent trying to imitate the wing-flapping movements of birds in an attempt to fly.

Free association

This is the most basic of all idea generation techniques (see Taylor, 1961). It does not rely upon force-fitting together two objectives to produce ideas, rather, one idea is used to generate another, which is then used to produce a third idea, and so on. Free association takes two forms:

1. Unstructured free association.
2. Structured free association.

In the first instance, unstructured free association, ideas are listed as they naturally occur where one idea leads to another. It typifies classical brainstorming. In the second case, structured free association tries to increase the relevance of ideas to a problem. In this latter case, the following procedures are followed:

1. A symbol – word, number, object, condition – that is directly related to the problem is drawn or otherwise recorded.
2. Whatever is suggested by the first step, whether or not it seems relevant to the problem, is recorded.
3. (2) is repeated until all possible associations have been listed.
4. Associations that seem to be most relevant to the problem are selected from the list.
5. The associations selected at (4) are used to develop and produce ideas that appear capable of solving the problem. The whole process from (1) is repeated if the process is unproductive.

Example
Imagine that the problem is how to reduce paperwork in the office. The starting symbol might be the word 'efficiency'. Associations might be: improve method, use computer, increased speed, less time, more leisure, more profitability, less cost, greater accuracy, more job satisfaction, more time to do important jobs, better decisions, fewer problems.

From this list we might select:

- ☐ Improve method – if one looks at what one is doing and questions the need it is often possible to perform a task in a different way, so that less paperwork is required.
- ☐ Use computers – they reduce the need for paper forms as information and reports can be stored, transmitted, received, read and acted upon.

A variant on the technique might be for a group of people to draw pictures on a round-robin basis with each picture providing a stimulation for the creation of the next.

Story writing

When we try to get to grips with an ill-structured problem we set about obtaining information that will increase our familiarity with the problem. Story writing (see Van Gundy, 1988) is a technique which helps this process along and at the same time helps to use the information to generate ideas.

Ideas are generated by writing a brief story that is somewhat related to the problem. Information in the story is then studied and is used for idea stimulation. The procedure is as follows:

1. A fictional story about the problem is developed (less than 1000 words). One should avoid writing directly about the problem and the story should be highly imaginative.
2. The story should then be examined closely and major principles, actions, characters, events, themes, expressions, objects, etc. should be listed.
3. This data should then be used as a basis for suggesting problem solutions.

Example
Problem: how to win a big contract with a major supplier?

Story: The car pulled slowly into the forecourt of the tall offices in Mayfair. A flunky strode majestically to open the door, an umbrella in his hand. The lightning flashed and momentarily the building was silhouetted against the dark evening sky. A clap of thunder welcomed Hermione as she crossed the pools shimmering in the cool of the night air.

The steps seemed endless; the doors never-ending; the typewriters clicking harder as the clock approached 4:30 p.m. The Christmas decorations created a brightness and a warmth that disguised the underlying austerity. Hermione smiled to herself – she too had been a typist, long ago.

A corner was turned and a large door was ajar. No sound issued from behind the door but in her mind Hermione could hear the rustle of papers rapidly scanned prior to the expected encounter. The door drew nearer; the pace slowed; one last thought on the opening gambit; should it involve a sacrifice in the opening that leads to positional advantage in exchange for material loss?

The next step involves picking out the relevant list of points:

1. pulled slowly
2. tall offices
3. Mayfair
4. flunky strode majestically
5. umbrella
6. clap of thunder
7. pools shimmering in the cool of the night air
8. steps seemed endless
9. the doors never-ending
10. the typewriters clicked harder as the clock approached 4:30
11. Christmas decorations created a brightness and a warmth
12. underlying austerity
13. Hermione
14. she too had been a typist, long ago
15. large door was ajar
16. rustle of papers
17. the door drew nearer
18. the pace slowed
19. opening gambit
20. should it involve a sacrifice in the opening that leads to positional advantage in exchange for material loss?

Next we take the list of points (1–20) raised and use them as a source of idea generation:

1. Take the process slowly and carefully – but not too slowly.

2. It's a tall order and needs a lot of consideration.
3. Likely to involve top level negotiation.
4. Look out for intermediaries who may look important but who only play a minor role.
5. Contingency plans are always required.
6. Those who shout loudest are likely to be effective.
7. Some things may look attractive but need to be on guard.
8. A long tiresome process – needs determination.
9. May be many people to see – time and time again.
10. Contracts are often won or lost during final stages of negotiation.
11. Atmosphere may seem friendly but underneath . . .
12. . . . it is very business-like.
13. Unusually sophisticated person to conduct negotiations required (possibly a woman).
14. Someone with a lot of experience of the business.
15. The opportunity definitely exists.
16. All documents are likely to be scrutinized meticulously.
17. Keep a watch on the final stages of negotiation.
18. Be deliberate during the final stages.
19. Need to pay attention to strategy to be employed.
20. Should it involve a sacrifice in the opening that leads to positional advantage in exchange for material loss? (the same as in the story).

Stories can also be written on a round-robin basis where each member of the group in turn adds a sentence. Another possibility is to have an independent person write a story and then simply work through the interpretational aspects oneself or as a group.

This is potentially a rich source of ideas and in most cases the stimuli will be sufficiently unrelated to permit the generation of unique ideas. It may also help to bring out insights that might have been overlooked by more conventional techniques.

Crawford slip writing

The idea was originated by C. C. Crawford in the 1920s and the variation here is that suggested by Charles C. Clark (1978). The procedure outlined is as follows:

1. Each person in a group (which can be several thousand people) receives a stack of at least 25 3″ × 5″ slips of paper.
2. A problem is presented verbally to the group using such expressions as: How can we . . .? or How to . . .?
3. Members of the group are required to record one idea on each slip of paper without thought being given to its relative importance.
4. The group is allowed to write for up to 10 minutes. At the end of this time the slips are collected in.
5. Another group of people then sort the ideas written on the slips into piles according to their frequency of occurrence or degree of usability.
6. Once the ideas have been sorted, the best ones are then developed into workable proposals.

Lotus blossom

This is a technique developed by the Japanese. It commences with a 'core thought' which forms the basis for the expansion of ideas into an ever-widening series of surrounding windows or petals. At the centre the core idea is surrounded by eight windows, each of which becomes the core thought for another set of eight windows. Each one of the core thoughts that is generated acts as the trigger mechanism for the subsequent set of eight new core thoughts which surround it (Figure 9.8).

Example
Suppose the core thought is: what staffing problems are there in the organization?
    The eight petals or windows surrounding this core thought would be found by brainstorming and might be:

1. More secretarial support.
2. Additional management trainees.
3. New blood from outside in some areas of middle management.
4. Continuous flow of sales staff on account of high turnover.
5. Apprentices for the workshops.
6. Skilled operatives in certain trades.
7. Part time cleaning and cooking staff.
8. More opportunities for disabled workers.

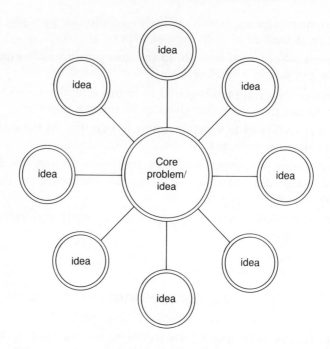

Figure 9.8 Lotus blossom.

Each of these ideas is then taken in turn and another eight ideas relating to each one are brainstormed. For example, 'Part time cleaning and cooking staff' could lead to:

1. Need to find new ways of recruiting part time cleaning staff.
2. Better conditions of service required for cooking staff.
3. Nursery/crèche facilities for all part time staff.
4. Transport facilities to be available for part time staff working unsocial hours.
5. Holiday entitlement needs to be reviewed, etc.

Lotus Blossom has something in common with mind-mapping techniques; in addition it relies on a novel way of representing ideas and their interrelationships visually. Lotus Blossom is especially useful for developing future scenarios.

Another example using Lotus Blossom might be:
Core thought: where do we want to be in 5 years' time?

1. Leaders in new technology.

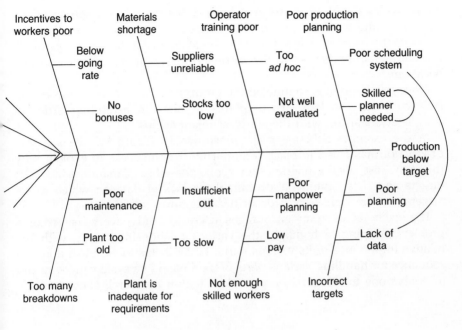

Figure 9.9 Fishbone diagram.

2. Highly profitable.
3. A company with an international reputation.
4. A global market leader.
5. Diversified.
6. etc.

'Leaders in new technology' could lead to:

1. Laser-guided control mechanisms, etc . . .

Fishbone diagram

The 'fishbone' diagram is attributed to Professor Ishikawa of Tokyo University (Majaro, 1991). Its purpose is to identify all possible causes contributing to a problem. As one can see from Figure 9.9, the shape of the structuring mechanism used resembles the shape of a fish's bone structure – hence fishbone diagram.

The process commences by placing the problem under consideration in a box, which denotes the shape of head of the fish. At the extremities of the bones and at 45 degrees to the backbone of the fish, every possible cause of the problem is listed. Further breakdowns of the causes are listed on additional branches of the bones running at 45 degrees to the backbone.

Once the diagram is completed the group use it as a discussion vehicle. It is customary to look at the points it raises in ascending order of complexity, starting with the simplest relationships.

In the example fishbone diagram shown in Figure 9.9 we see that production has failed to reach target. The diagram seeks to explain why this is the case. As the diagram shows, one possible explanation is incorrect targets and these might be attributable to lack of data on which to set targets (bottom right-hand side of the diagram).

The fishbone diagram encourages users to study every aspect of a problem, helping to highlight the various relationships along with the relative importance of its various parts. It also helps to establish a logical sequence for handling various parts of a problem in a systematic way and to enable one to see parts of a problem within its overall context.

Scenario writing

Scenario writing is a tool which has its origins in long-term planning and technological forecasting. Here, the interest has always been very much in speculating how the future is going to develop and, in particular, what future impact the development of new technologies is likely to have on the demand for goods and services.

Scenario writing is a systematic way of looking into the future and forces an organization's management team to be receptive to the need for change and creative thinking. It is the experience of considering new possibilities and opening up one's mind to considering what might happen, rather than the accuracy of any predictions, which is of greatest benefit.

The exercise is a team one where there is a leader–facilitator who introduces the session and coordinates the final session. The leader–facilitator also coordinates the preparation of the final report. Team members are referred to as 'scenario writers' and each one is an expert in his particular field. The types of experts who participate in the exercise will be related to the activities and concerns of the organization. The procedure adopted is as follows:

1. *Briefing* – here all scenario writers are requested to consider what developments will take place in their area of specialization over the next

5–10 years. They are also asked to provide supporting evidence for this and to assess the likely impact of these developments upon the organization.

2. *Individual scenario writing* – scenario writers spend up to 2 weeks preparing their individual scenarios independently.

3. *Collective scenario writing* – here the scenario writers meet up to present their individual papers and viewpoints and to reach a consensus viewpoint on possible developments. The output of this meeting is eventually a report produced by the team and coordinated by the leader–facilitator.

Scenario writing is a very productive exercise when the situation under review is a complex one requiring consideration by experts. It is, however, an extremely time-consuming exercise and so tends not to be undertaken frequently in the work situation because of pressure of time.

Scenario day-dreaming

This method is like scenario writing in so far as it, too, tries to look into the future and assess trends which are likely to have an impact on the organization. It is, however, a less formal kind of exercise and a written report is *not* produced. Everything is undertaken on a verbal basis and the sessions can be completed comfortably over the course of a couple of days. Scenario day-dreamers are not asked to substantiate their contributions nor do they have to undertake research or produce individual written reports. The method aims to stimulate people's imaginations, to think in a broader context and to consider more unusual ideas.

It is usual to hold the 2-day session away from the place of work at a conference centre or some similar venue. Ideally, eight to ten contributors make a good group size, but much depends on the size of the organization and the complexity of the business. In some cases fewer participants will be the norm, whereas in others more participants will be necessary.

Once again there is a leader–facilitator whose role is to plan the sessions in detail, advise on the selection of participants, brief participants about the sessions, lead the sessions, motivate and stimulate the group during the sessions and help to summarize the conclusions which result from the sessions. It is also useful if one member of the group keeps minutes of the proceedings. Alternatively, this task could be delegated to an additional party member who acts as scribe. The procedure adopted for the session is given below.

Preparation

The leader informs people about the nature of the session and its purpose in advance, stressing the need to be open-minded and positive throughout the forthcoming session.

The scenario day-dreaming session

The session must be carefully divided into manageable sections, with a beginning, middle and end. During the opening session participants should make themselves known to one another, the leader should explain what is going to happen and any queries that members have should be dealt with. A warm-up session should also be conducted to get participants into the mode of the technique. The topic chosen does not need to be related to the work of the organization.

Following the warm-up session one moves on to the scenario day-dreaming proper. The first step in the proceedings is to identify the various factors which are likely to influence the future success of the company. Factors such as economic trends, cost of commodities, developments in politics and government, changes in demography, changes in the law, technological change, changes in social structure, changes in customer requirements and competitor activities need to be considered. The idea is to identify and put priorities on the most important factors (see cross-impact matrix in the next section) and to get participants really engrossed and involved in what they are doing. Once the main factors have been identified for consideration they should be summarized on a flip-chart in order of priority.

Once this is done the group is in a position to start the process of scenario day-dreaming. The group needs to split into syndicates with not less than three people and the afternoon of the first day and morning of the second day should be put aside for this purpose. Each one of the groups is given several of the previously identified important factors to consider. The purpose is to consider each factor in considerable depth and arrive at a future scenario for each one. In setting up the groups care has to be taken to ensure that group members with the requisite ability and experience are chosen to deal with the factors that are assigned to each group. Syndicates should spend roughly half an hour to produce a scenario for each factor they have been asked to consider.

During the afternoon of the second day the group reassembles to hear the syndicates' presentations of individual scenarios. The entire group as a whole discusses each scenario in turn and tries to reach a consensus about the likely scenario for each factor. When all the scenarios have been dealt with in this way the group then has to integrate the scenarios into a single, comprehensive vision of the future. This is done under the direction of the group leader.

	Strengths S	Weaknesses W
Opportunities O	Strategies (S–O) Maximize on strengths and opportunities	Strategies (W–O) Minimize on weaknesses but maximize on opportunities
Threats T	Strategies (S–T) Maximize on strengths but minimize on threats	Strategies (W–T) Minimize on weaknesses and threats

Figure 9.10 The TOWS matrix.

Generating ideas in response to the scenario

Once again syndicates are formed in order to consider the agreed future scenario and to get ideas on how the organization can respond to the opportunities and threats that are involved. Other creative techniques, such as brainstorming and the TOWS matrix (Weihrich, 1982) (Figure 9.10), may be used at this particular point.

The TOWS matrix presents a mechanism for facilitating the linkage between company strengths and weaknesses and threats and opportunities in the market-place. It also provides a framework for identifying and formulating strategies. In the first place threats, opportunities, strengths and weaknesses are identified and listed in the appropriate cells of the grid. Next, combinations of strengths and opportunities, weaknesses and threats, weaknesses and opportunities, strengths with threats are examined in order to generate possible strategies. It should be noted that in generating strategies one maximizes strengths and opportunities and minimizes weaknesses and threats, as shown in the cells in the figure.

For example, the entry to one cell of the grid could involve maximizing opportunities and maximizing strengths. This would amount to putting together at least one strength and one opportunity to produce a strategy that capitalizes upon this combination. Brainstorming can be used in conjunction with the matrix to generate strategies based upon the identified threats, opportunities, weaknesses and strengths.

Closing session

The whole group reconvenes and the leader reviews the proceedings, summarizing how the group sees matters developing and how the organization can try to meet future challenges.

Applications for scenario day-dreaming

This is a technique which is useful where a longer-term perspective is required. Suitable applications include:

Strategic business units

	Present B1	B2	B3	Proposed B10	B11	Potential B20	B21	Impact +	−
Customers									
Segment A	0	3	0	4	−3	0	1	8	−3
Segment B	0	0	4	0	0	3	−3	7	−3
Competitors									
Actual A1	0	−2	0	−1	0	0	−2	0	−5
Potential P1	−4	−2	0	0	0	−4	−1	0	−11
Technology T1	2	0	−3	0	1	4	0	7	−3
Regulations R1	0	0	2	0	−3	0	−2	2	−5
Economic trends ET1	0	3	3	−1	0	−4	0	6	−5
Cultural trends CT1	−1	2	3	0	4	1	0	10	−1
Demographic trend DT1	0	0	2	0	−2	0	0	2	−2
Total +	2	8	14	4	5	8	1		
Total −	−5	−4	−3	−2	−8	−8	−8		

Impact scale

Threats						Opportunities
−4 −3 −2 −1			0			+1 +2 +3 +4
High negative impact			No impact			High positive impact

Figure 9.11 Cross-impact matrix (Aaker, 1988).

□ defining an organization's mission statement; and
□ determining strategies which will help to maintain or improve a firm's position *vis-à-vis* competition.

Cross-impact analysis

Cross-impact analysis helps in examining the impact that a mixture of external threats and opportunities can have on the undertakings of an organization. In implementing the technique one has to obtain data from a range of sources including customers, competitors, the market and the environment. The procedure involves assessing the impact that changes or trends in these factors are likely to have on present, proposed or potential activities of the organization. Anything that threatens the prosperity of the organization is viewed as having a negative effect on the establishment, while opportunities are reasoned to have positive effects.

The various impacts are recorded on a grid (see Figure 9.11) and on a scale ranging from +4 to −4, where 0 specifies a lack of impact. The sum of various extraneous threats and opportunities on each one of the identified business–organizational activities is then noted. In addition the total scores of opportunities and threats facing each activity of the organization are recorded. All ratings are a matter of the subjective opinions of executives.

The cross-impact matrix is useful as a stand-alone tool in its own right but is also an invaluable tool when conducting scenario day-dreaming, as it helps to pick out the environmental factors which are important and provides a ranking for them (see above).

References

Aaker, D. (1988) *Strategic Market Management*, New York: Wiley.

Clark, C. C. (1978) *The Crawford Slip Writing Method*, Kent, OH: Charles H. Clark.

Goman, C. G. (1989) *Creative Thinking in Business*, London: Kogan Page.

Gordon, W. J. J. (1961) *Synectics*, New York: Harper & Row.

Hicks, M. J. (1991) *Problem Solving in Business and Management*, London: Chapman & Hall.

Koberg, D. and Bagnall, J. (1976) *The Universal Trader*, Los Altos, CA: William Kaufmann Inc.

Majaro, S. (1991) *The Creative Marketer*, Oxford: Butterworth Heinemann.

Marquis, D. G. (1969) 'The anatomy of successful innovations', *Innovations*, November.

Taylor, J. W. (1961) *How to Create Ideas*, Englewood Cliffs, NJ: Prentice Hall.

Van Gundy, A. B. (1988) *Techniques of Structured Problem Solving*, New York: Van Nostrand Reinhold.

Weihrich, H. (1982) 'The TOWS matrix: a tool for situational analysis', *Long Range Planning*, **15**(2), 54–66.

10

Evaluating ideas

Although creative problem solving is primarily concerned with producing different insights or perspectives on a problem, from a pragmatic point of view owners of problems are looking for solutions. Creative problem-solving techniques will produce many possible solutions but it may well be that only one or a few of these solutions can be implemented; the task is to decide which solutions to adopt. Evaluation of ideas is therefore about finding the best solutions to a problem.

Sometimes it may be relatively easy to identify which is the best solution. Where only a few solutions have been generated and it is fairly obvious that one of them is better than any of the others, then the task of choosing is straightforward. It is often the case, however, that many possible solutions will have been generated and that it will not be at all clear which is the best one. Moreover, if there is scope to implement several ideas it will be necessary to select the best ideas from those that have been produced. It is under these circumstances that we need to make use of evaluation methods, such as those which are described in this chapter.

Collating and sorting ideas

We all know from trying to put together a jigsaw puzzle how difficult it is to do unless we sort pieces in the first place. If the jigsaw is an outdoor scene then we will collect together all the pieces on which there is sky, all the pieces on which there is grass, all the pieces on which there are trees, all the straight-edged pieces, etc. Sorting pieces with characteristics in common into piles is a good way of preparing oneself for fitting the pieces of the jigsaw together. The same kind of reasoning applies when

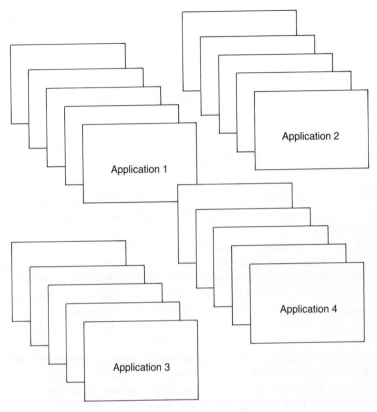

Figure 10.1 Collating ideas on cards by application.

we have generated a large number of ideas and want to evaluate them.

Once ideas have been generated it is necessary to collate the ideas prior to evaluating them. One seldom has the resources available to implement all the ideas one generates and, of course, where ideas are substitutes for one another then not all the ideas can be implemented. Before one can evaluate ideas they need to be collated so that duplicate ideas can be discarded. Where many ideas have been generated, grouping the ideas into clusters also makes it easier to rank the ideas, in the first instance, so that the best ones in the clusters can then be evaluated *vis-à-vis* one another.

Majaro (1991) proposes a diagram like a spider's web to help in the process. Where many ideas are concerned the web may become rather complex and unwieldy. A simple way of sorting and collating ideas can be achieved with the use of small cards. Individual ideas are recorded on each card. The cards are then sorted into groupings according to the general application or nature of the ideas (see Figure 10.1).

For example, suppose one had just brainstormed ideas relating to what to do with a particular byproduct from an industrial process: the brainstorming session will have produced a fairly large number of ideas in a random order. Inspection of the ideas generated may identify a number of different and distinct application categories. Ideas are written on cards and sorted into groupings according to the application categories.

Evaluating ideas

Once ideas have been sorted a mechanism has to be found that allows one to rank ideas and choose the ones that appear to be most desirable for implementation.

Sometimes the ideas generated can be evaluated fairly easily. Some may stand out as much more suitable solutions to identified problems than others. On other occasions we may want to try out several possible ideas and ranking is not particularly important. At other times, however, we may generate several or even many ideas and considerable uncertainty may exist with respect to which idea is to be preferred over another. In a situation where we have scarce resources and where it is desirable to implement a small proportion, or even only one, of the ideas we have generated then some method of ranking the ideas is desirable.

The simplest method of evaluating ideas involves constructing tables which allow us to compare the advantages and disadvantages of the various ideas. For example, suppose we have three ideas on how to move into a new product market. They might be:

1. Acquire a specialist small firm already operating in the market.
2. Form a strategic alliance with a firm which has access to the same market with other products.
3. Develop the necessary product internally and train existing marketing and sales teams to market the product.

First we list criteria against which we want to evaluate the ideas. The same criteria are used for each of the three options and space is left to indicate whether the idea was rated as having predominantly advantages or disadvantages on those criteria (see Table 10.1).

As a rough evaluation tool this technique may be useful. In the above example, idea 2 seems to have the better rating. However, except for possible use as a preliminary screening device this method has little merit as an approach to idea evaluation. Its main weakness lies in its assumption that all the criteria are equal in weight.

Table 10.1 Cross-impact table

Criteria	Idea 1		Idea 2		Idea 3	
	Advantages	Disadvantages	Advantages	Disadvantages	Advantages	Disadvantages
Impact on						
Sales	×		×		×	
Profits	×		×			×
Cashflow		×	×			×
New investment required		×	×			×
Risk		×	×			×
Company objectives	×		×		×	
Score	3	3	6	0	2	4

More sophisticated screening methods have been suggested by Hamilton (1974). The methods involve 'culling' ideas which fail to satisfy key criteria and rating and scoring ideas against desirable criteria. Many decisions are taken in a group situation and techniques which are specifically designed to take account of this include the 'Castle technique', suggested by O'Rourke (1984).

Culling, rating and scoring screens

Culling screens
Criteria are developed that can be answered with a 'yes' or 'no' response. Ideas receiving a 'no' response to any of the culling criteria are eliminated.

Rating screens
Criteria are developed that can be answered with a 'yes' or 'no' response. Each 'yes' scores 1. each 'no' scores 0. A minimal passing score is established for the set of criteria. An idea falling below the minimum score for rating criteria is eliminated.

Scoring screens
Criteria are developed that can be answered with a rating response such as poor (1), fair (2) or good (3). Each criterion also receives a weighting – the more important the criterion the greater the weighting. Each idea is rated against each criterion and a weighted score assigned for each

Table 10.2 Scoring screen

Criterion	Poor	Fair	Good	Weight	Total
A	1	2	3	2	6
B	1	2	3	3	6
C	+	2	3	3	3
Minimum score is 17			Pass ...		Reject X

criterion it is rated against. The totals of the weighted criterion scores are then summed. A minimal passing score is established for the set of criteria. An idea falling below the minimum score for rating criteria is eliminated (see Table 10.2).

The Castle technique

The Castle technique comprises five steps:

1. Establish a time limit – perhaps an hour.
2. Tell those involved in the evaluation that there will be three criteria used to evaluate each idea:
   □ acceptability (the extent to which it satisfies existing goals);
   □ practicality (the extent to which it satisfies financial and time constraints); and
   □ originality (the extent to which it makes a significant improvement on the status quo).
3. Each idea then has to be numbered and participants in the evaluation exercise are given the same number of votes as there are ideas (for example, if there are 30 ideas, each person receives 30 votes). Participants are then instructed to vote for each idea with either a 'yes' or a 'no' vote. One vote per idea per individual is allowed.
4. Voting then takes place.
5. The two ideas which receive the highest number of positive votes (number of 'yes' votes – number of 'no' votes) are then combined into one idea.

The Castle technique is both simple to use and implement.

Other useful evaluation methods include 'creative evaluation', suggested by Moore (1962), 'decision balance sheet', developed by Janis and

Mann (1977), 'disjointed incrementalism', attributable to Braybrooke and Lindblom (1963), 'reverse brainstorming', described by Whiting (1958), and 'weighting systems'.

Creative evaluation

This is most useful when dealing with a large number of ideas. Creative evaluation tries to present ideas in a format that will reduce the amount of time required for evaluation. All ideas are evaluated in terms of their time and money requirements, as follows:

1. A list of the ideas is assembled.
2. Ideas are categorized into three groups:
   (a) simple
   (b) hard
   (c) difficult
   Simple ideas are defined as those which can be put into action with a minimum of expenditure on time and money; hard ideas require more expenditure, while difficult ideas require the most expenditure.
3. Ideas and their categories are then passed on to management for additional evaluation.

Creative evaluation is perhaps most appropriate for a cursory examination of a large number of ideas.

Decision balance sheet

The decision balance sheet (Figure 10.2) requires an analysis of each idea with respect to four criteria:

1. Tangible gains and losses for self.
2. Tangible gains and losses for others.
3. Self-approval or self-disapproval – degree of self-satisfaction or otherwise.
4. Social approval or disapproval – degree of approval or otherwise by others.

The steps involved are:

1. List all the ideas.

losses.............

		Positive associations +	Negative associations −
1. Tangible gains and losse for self	+ −		
2. Tangible gains and losses for others	+ −		
3. Self-approval or self-disapproval	+ −		
4. Social approval or disapproval	+ −		

Figure 10.2   Decision balance sheet.

2. Rank ideas in terms of personal preferences.

3. Take the top two ideas and write down the positive and negative points of each along with any other points you think might be relevant in evaluating the ideas you have.

4. For each idea that has been generated, a balance sheet grid has to be constructed. It should contain twelve cells arranged into three columns and four rows.

5. Using the positive and negative features identified for the two ideas in (3), fill in a separate grid for each idea. Next, complete the sheets for the remaining alternatives.

6. Review all the sheets that have been completed and include any other considerations that are necessary.

7. Develop a list of pertinent considerations through reading the literature or consulting experts.

8. Group the pertinent considerations into the four category areas and examine the list to discover whether any new gains or losses might be suggested.

9. Employing a 7-point scale ranging from hardly important (1) to extremely important (7), rate each of the considerations within each cell of every balance sheet.

10. Review all the balance sheets and rank ideas in order of preference.

11. When a decision has to be made select the best alternative for implementation.

Disjointed incrementalism

This method contrasts with the rational approach applied in most problem-solving models. In applying disjointed incrementalism both a current and a desired state of events are identified and then a means is sought to achieve the objectives in the case of the rational approach. An important feature of the rational model is the attempt made to consider every possible relevant alternative and then rationally select the alternative with the best potential for solving the problem.

The disjointed incrementalist approach is somewhat different. Objectives in policy analysis are often poorly defined and constantly changing. This makes the rational model inappropriate. Alternatives are not evaluated by establishing whether one of them is of more use than another. One simply asks whether an increment in one value is desirable and if so whether any of the increments can be traded for an increment of another alternative.

Thus, we do not seek to ascertain whether strikes are preferred less than salary increases, but how much in terms of salaries could be sacrificed to avert strikes. It is therefore not necessary to list all possible alternatives and rank them carefully according to their absolute differences. The steps involved are:

1. Determine the consequences of the present state of the problem.
2. List the alternatives known or expected to be different from each other incrementally, and from the present state of the problem.
3. Rank in order the alternatives in terms of preferences, according to the degree of incrementalism by which the alternatives differ.
4. Resolve conflicts between alternative preferences by stating how much of one value is worth sacrificing to achieve an increment of another.

This kind of approach often leads to the alleviation of a problem rather than its resolution.

Goalstorming

The essence of management responsibility is setting goals and getting colleagues involved in doing their jobs. Goalstorming makes use of this principle and is particularly effective when there is evidence of vested interests at stake, making a consensus difficult to achieve. The steps are as follows:

1. State the primary objective.

2. Enumerate the secondary goals relating to the primary objective.

3. Subdivide the secondary goals.

4. Rank all the subdivided goals as follows:
    (a) Randomly select two goals and decide which one is the more important.
    (b) Repeat the process of randomly selecting and comparing goals until all goals have been evaluated.
    (c) Based on the comparison, rank the goals in order of importance.

For example, suppose the primary objective is to reduce the cost of making sales calls. Secondary goals might be: increase the sales to call ratio; reduce the percentage of unproductive calls; reduce the time spent travelling between calls; etc. Subdividing the secondary goals, in the case of reducing the percentage of unproductive calls, might amount to such things as improving the quality of prospect lists, improving the quality of pre-call telephone introductions, etc.

When ranking goals it is necessary to follow the following guidelines:

(a) Evaluation of the relative importance of any one goal must be unanimous.

(b) Decisions on the importance of any one goal over another should not be changed later.

(c) Difficult decisions can sometimes be resolved by subdividing the goal in question and comparing the subdivisions to the other goal.

(d) Some goals can be combined with others to increase their importance.

(e) If any ranking changes are required the whole process *must* be repeated.

Highlighting

This is a relatively efficient idea evaluation and selection technique developed by Firestien and Treffinger (1983). It involves combining idea 'hits' into 'hotspots' which are then modified and turned into workable solutions. The steps are as follows:

1. Ideas should be consecutively numbered and arrayed in a list. This should be examined and any that look interesting should be marked

(hits). These ideas should be selected, regardless of whether they have workable application.

2. Clusters of hits that appear to be related to one another should be identified as hotspots. The ideas for each identified hotspot should be listed.
3. Each of the hotspots should be reviewed and a note made of what it seems to represent. These descriptions can deal with general meanings, implications and possible consequences of each.
4. Select one hotspot that seems to best satisfy the needs of the problem. This forms the solution. If it is appropriate, two or more hotspots may be combined to produce a solution.

This is a simple and most effective way of evaluating and selecting ideas. Virtually no training is required and because of its open-ended nature, it allows for plenty of discussion when used in a group situation.

Reverse brainstorming

Reverse brainstorming was invented by the Hotpoint Company as a group method for discovering all possible weaknesses of an idea and anticipating what might go wrong when the idea is implemented (Whiting, 1958). It is very similar to classical brainstorming except that *criticisms* instead of *ideas* are generated. As such it is a method for evaluating ideas. The procedure is as follows:

1. The same people who generate the ideas are usually called upon to evaluate them.
2. The objective or problem along with the list of ideas generated are written on a flip-chart and then displayed in a prominent position.
3. The first idea on the list is then criticized by one or other members of the group and a note of the idea along with the criticism is recorded on the flip-chart.
4. When all criticisms of the first idea have been exhausted, the group starts to criticize the second idea and the process continues until all the ideas have been criticized.
5. Following classical brainstorming procedures, the group then re-examines the ideas to generate possible solutions for each identified weakness.
6. The idea that possesses the fewest number of weaknesses and that will be most likely to solve the problem is selected for implementation.

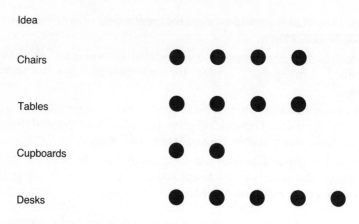

Idea

Chairs

Tables

Cupboards

Desks

Which furniture should the company manufacture first?
The sticking dots say desks

Figure 10.3 Sticking dots.

Often, brainstorming sessions generate many different ideas. Reverse brainstorming, however, will not be suitable when there are more than eight to ten ideas to evaluate. Reverse brainstorming is a more useful technique to use with a small number of ideas that have survived an initial screening process.

Sticking dots

This is a useful method to employ when a small group of individuals is trying to evaluate ideas (Geschka, 1979). It involves allowing each group member to have a fixed number of votes (usually these are physically represented in the form of self-adhesive, coloured dots) (Figure 10.3). Members can then vote in any way they wish. The steps are as follows:

1. Ideas that have already been generated are displayed on flip-charts or cards that are pinned to a large wallboard.
2. Each member of the group has a card on which there are adhesive dots of one colour, unique to that person. The number of dots corresponds to 10 per cent of the total number of ideas listed on the board.
3. Ideas are evaluated by members sticking dots next to the ideas they prefer. Dots may be allocated in any manner. A person may allocate all his or her allocated dots against one idea if he or she desires.

Table 10.3 Weighted scores

Criterion	Weight	Option 1		Option 2	
		Score (max. 9)	Weighted Score	Score (max. 9)	Weighted Score
a	0.15	7	1.05	6	0.90
b	0.20	4	0.80	7	1.40
c	0.15	3	0.45	5	0.75
d	0.30	5	1.50	3	0.90
e	0.20	6	1.20	7	1.40
	1.00		5.00		5.35

4. The ideas receiving the largest number of votes are selected for further analysis or implementation.

Weighting systems

If there is a need to choose from two or more options a common procedure is to assign weights to the different evaluation criteria. Since not all criteria are likely to be valued equally, such a procedure provides a systematic method for assessing the strengths and weaknesses of each option.

The normal procedure for most weighting methods is to produce a list of evaluation criteria, assign weights to the criteria, rate each alternative against the criteria, and then to select the option that best satisfies the criteria. This might be done as shown in Table 10.3.

Five criteria are identified and the group assigns weights to the importance of the criterion as shown (averaged out across the group). Scores are then assigned to the two options against each criterion in turn and averaged out for the group. Multiplying the score against the criterion by weight assigned to the criterion in each case and summing across all criteria produces the total weighted score for each of the options. In this case option 2 would seem to be preferred.

Multifactor matrix

A useful screening device to cull out the weak ideas and identify the strong ideas is to use an extension of the weighting system idea known as a 'multifactor matrix'.

Table 10.4 Allocation of marks by one executive

Compatibility with firm's requirements		Idea attractiveness	
Attribute (1)	22 marks	Attribute (1)	47 marks
Attribute (2)	24 marks	Attribute (2)	11 marks
Attribute (3)	33 marks	Attribute (3)	16 marks
Attribute (4)	21 marks	Attribute (4)	26 marks
Total	100 marks	Total	100 marks

A multifactor matrix considers two broad categories. Across the horizontal axis is idea attractiveness and along the vertical axis, compatibility with the firm's requirements. The general categories of idea attractiveness and compatibility with the firm's requirements permit additional factors to be considered in positioning ideas in the matrix.

Constructing a matrix

We will work through the rating of a single idea and use each one of two sets of four attributes for the two dimensions of compatibility with the firm's requirements and idea attractiveness mentioned above.

First, one would need to have executives in the organization indicate weights that should be attached to the two groups of attributes. This would be done by requesting the executives to take each set of four attributes at a time and divide a hundred marks between the four attributes to reflect the degree of importance of each one of the attributes. By way of illustration, one executive might allocate the marks as shown in Table 10.4.

It will be assumed that there are five executives in the organization, and that we request each one to do this exercise. When the task is completed, we aggregate the marks given by every executive for each one of the attributes in turn. Next, the total number of marks allocated to every attribute, in turn, is divided by 5 so the average number of marks allocated by the executives to every one of the attributes can be established. Suppose the results appear as in Table 10.5.

To obtain the weights for individual attributes we have to divide by 100, since the weights by definition must add up to one (Table 10.6).

The next step is ask each one of the five executives to rate the idea against each one of the two sets of four attributes on a scale running from 0 to 9. We then calculate the average rating (by dividing the aggregate ratings for each attribute by 5) for the idea against each of the two sets of attributes. Suppose the results appear as in Table 10.7.

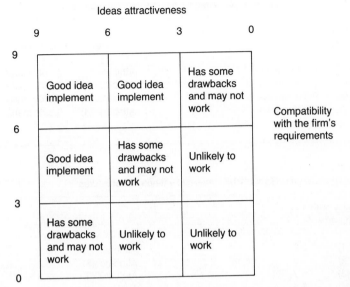

Figure 10.4 Idea attractiveness: compatibility with requirements matrix.

Table 10.5 Average number of marks allocated by all executives

Compatibility with firm's requirements		Idea attractiveness	
Attribute (1)	18.5 marks	Attribute (1)	36.6 marks
Attribute (2)	26.6 marks	Attribute (2)	15.5 marks
Attribute (3)	31.8 marks	Attribute (3)	15.2 marks
Attribute (4)	23.1 marks	Attribute (4)	32.7 marks
Total	100 marks	Total	100 marks

We then obtain the weighted scores by multiplying by the relevant weight assigned to every attribute (Table 10.8).

The idea's position on the grid can then be plotted as shown in Table 10.9.

In this particular case, the idea seems to be reasonably attractive. Any ideas which fall into the top left-hand three cells will be good ideas as far as the firm is concerned. The matrix shown in Figure 10.4 and Table 10.10 suggests action that might be taken according to where the positioning of the idea within the matrix occurs.

Table 10.6 Weights for individual attributes

Compatibility with firm's requirements		Idea attractiveness	
Attribute (1)	0.185 marks	Attribute (1)	0.366 marks
Attribute (2)	0.266 marks	Attribute (2)	0.155 marks
Attribute (3)	0.318 marks	Attribute (3)	0.152 marks
Attribute (4)	0.231 marks	Attribute (4)	0.327 marks
Total	1	Total	1

Table 10.7 Average ratings for attributes

Compatibility with firm's requirements		Idea attractiveness	
Attribute (1)	3.2	Attribute (1)	5.6
Attribute (2)	4.8	Attribute (2)	8.2
Attribute (3)	6.7	Attribute (3)	7.3
Attribute (4)	5.5	Attribute (4)	7.5

Table 10.8 Calculation of weighted scores

Compatibility with firm's requirements		Idea attractiveness	
Attribute (1) $0.185 \times 3.2 = 0.59$		Attribute (1) $0.366 \times 5.6 = 2.05$	
Attribute (2) $0.266 \times 4.8 = 1.28$		Attribute (2) $0.155 \times 8.2 = 1.27$	
Attribute (3) $0.318 \times 6.7 = 2.13$		Attribute (3) $0.152 \times 7.3 = 1.11$	
Attribute (4) $0.231 \times 5.5 = 1.27$		Attribute (4) $0.327 \times 7.5 = 2.45$	
Total	5.27	Total	6.88

Table 10.9 An idea positioned on the grid

		High	Medium	Low	
	High				9
Idea attractiveness		6.88 – – –> ×			
	Medium		∧		6
			.		3
	Low		.		
			.		0
		9	6 5.27	3	

Table 10.10 Strategies and grid position

	High	Medium	Low	
High				9
	Develop	Develop	Discard	
				6
Medium	Develop	Try to modify	Discard	
Attractiveness				3
Low	Try to modify	Try to modify	Discard	
				0
	9	6	3	

Choosing an evaluation method

In this chapter we have considered a variety of techniques for evaluating ideas. These range from the very simple to the quite complex. When choosing an appropriate method one should examine the advantages and disadvantages of each in relationship to the problem which is being studied so that an appropriate choice can be made. Thus, while reverse brainstorming may seem an appealing method it may not be suitable for all kinds of problems. Indeed, it may be that more than one method may need to be applied. This is particularly the case where an evaluation by reverse brainstorming produces a number of attractive options, but where it is difficult to differentiate between their various appeals and to put them into some kind of rank order. Under such circumstances a rating procedure may be required to enable the various options to be ranked.

In other circumstances, of course, it may be possible to select from a range of options without having recourse to simple or elaborate evaluation models such as those we have discussed above. If this is the case then one should not feel that it is a requirement that an evaluation model should be used.

References

Braybrooke, D. and Lindblom, C. E. (1963) *A Strategy of Decision*, New York: The Free Press.

Firestien, R. L. and Treffinger, D. J. (1983) 'Ownership and converging: essential ingredients of Creative Problem Solving', *Journal of Creative Behaviour*, **17**(1), 32–8.

Geschka, H. (1979) 'Methods and organisation of idea generation', Paper presented at the Creativity Development week II, Center for Creative Leadership, Greensboro, North Carolina, September.

Hamilton, H. R. (1974) 'Screening business development opportunities', *Business Horizon*, August, 13–24.

Janis, I. L. and Mann, L. (1977) 'Decision making: a psychological analysis of conflict', in I. L. Janis and L. Mann, *Choice and Commitment*, New York: The Free Press.

Moore, L. B. (1962) 'Creative action – the evaluation, development, and use of ideas', in S. J. Parnes and H. F. Harding (eds), *A Sourcebook for Creative Thinking*, New York: Scribner.

O'Rourke, P. J. (1984) *The Castle Technique: How to achieve group consensus in a very short time with no argument*, Lyons, CO: Steamboat Valley Press.

Whiting, C. S. (1958) *Creative Thinking*, New York: Van Nostrand Reinhold.

11

Implementing ideas

Defining problems, generating insights and evaluating ideas are only part of the task of problem solving. Even when it seems that a solution to a problem has been found there is still the onerous task of getting solutions or ideas adopted. Putting ideas into practice can be difficult, especially when there are obstacles to prevent their introduction. Getting over these obstacles represents the final stage in the problem-solving process. One of the main factors which should be taken into account when evaluating ideas is the ease with which an idea can be implemented, and when establishing criteria against which to evaluate solutions or ideas this should be taken into account.

Blocks to getting ideas adopted

Blocks to implementation reflect such things as a lack of adequate resources to implement ideas, a lack of commitment and motivation in those required to implement ideas, resistance to change, procedural obstacles, perceived risk associated with implementing ideas, political undercurrents, lack of cooperation in the organization or a feeling of distrust, and so on (Figure 11.1).

The key is to discover in the first place what resistance is likely to be encountered and what the reasons for such resistance are. Armed with such information one can then tailor solutions so that the resistance encountered is reduced. The ethos and atmosphere of the organization are often a pointer towards whether difficulties might be encountered when trying to introduce change.

Figure 11.2 lists a series of responses that one might conceivably obtain

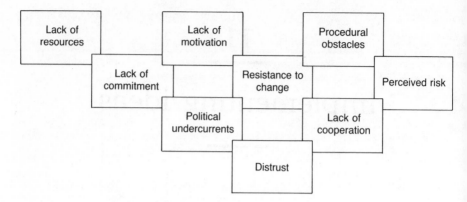

Figure 11.1 Sources of resistance to new idea.

when trying to introduce change, new ideas or solutions to problems into an organization. Some of the responses are positive and encouraging while others are negative, and suggest that there may well be resistance to be encountered. If the latter is the case then preparatory work will have to be carried out within the organization before the change of idea can be implemented.

Human and technological factors give rise to implementation blocks. Some of the blocks are intentional and are devised to serve as checks to ensure that the organization always operates smoothly. Other blocks are unintentional and arise from the peculiar historical development of the organization. There is also a third type of block that operates independently of the organization's internal processes. An example of this last kind of impediment is a change in market demand that can prevent idea implementation.

When evaluating ideas one should always take into account the likelihood of implementation blocks. Simply recognizing the existence of various blocks can lead to trade-offs being made among the available alternatives.

The identification of possible blocks can be assisted by considering the following questions:

☐ Are the resources available sufficient to allow implementation of an idea?

☐ Is it likely that those who will be required to implement the idea will have sufficient motivation to do so?

☐ Is the idea likely to encounter 'closed thinking' or a general resistance to change?

When faced with trying to bring about change, are the
people with whom you are dealing most likely to say:

1. Can we ask questions? [ ]
2. We've tried it before [ ]
3. It would take too long [ ]
4. Excuse us but we don't really understand that [ ]
5. Is this what you had in mind? [ ]
6. That's not my job [ ]
7. How could we improve things? [ ]
8. What have we overlooked? [ ]
9. We don't do things that way here [ ]
10. Who else would be affected by the change? [ ]
11. What would happen if . . .? [ ]
12. It's impossible [ ]
13. You may be right but . . . [ ]
14. Who else has a suggestion? [ ]
15. What ideas have you come up with? [ ]
16. Why do we always do it like that? [ ]
17. My mind is definitely made up on the matter [ ]
18. I don't think that it's important [ ]
19. It's good enough [ ]
20. We don't have time just now [ ]

Place a √ in the appropriate boxes

Score −1 each time if a tick has been put in boxes:
2, 3, 6, 9, 12, 13, 17, 18, 19, 20 and total score

Interpretation

High resistance   −7 to −10
Considerable resistance −3 to −6
Little resistance   −1 to −2
No resistance   0

Figure 11.2 Assessing resistance to change when implementing ideas.

□ Are there procedural obstacles present in the organization that need to be overcome before the idea can be implemented?

□ Are there structural obstacles in the organization that need to be overcome?

□ Are there organizational or managerial policies that need to be overcome?

□ Is risk-taking likely to be tolerated in implementing an idea? If so, how much risk-taking?

□ Are there organizational politics at work that might prevent an idea from being implemented?

□ Is the general atmosphere of the organization conducive to cooperation and hence eases the process of implementing an idea?

Putting ideas into practice

A variety of tools or techniques exist which can be used profitably to help introduce new ideas in a systematic and planned way into an organizational setting. 'Consensus mapping', suggested by Hart and others (1985) is one such tool. It helps participants to visualize, analyze and organize ideas that are sequence dependent. In applying the technique a graphic map is created which portrays ideas in relationship to one another and shows how they are thought to be interdependent. Another useful method suggested by Kepner and Tregoe (1976) is 'potential problem analysis'. This latter technique emphasizes a systematic approach for anticipating problems that are likely to prevent a project from being implemented. PERT networks and Research Planning Diagrams are also useful tools for helping to implement newly generated ideas which involve a substantial time scale for implementation.

In addition to the systematic planning and introduction of ideas, there is the task of persuading people who are going to make use of those ideas that they are worth using. Ideas may have to be sold to people who can authorize their implementation. This may ease the task of gaining subsequent motivation to ensure that the new ideas are successful after they have been adopted. Putting ideas into practice usually requires four things (Figure 11.3):

1. An ability to get people to accept ideas in the first place.
2. Being able to cope with difficult obstacles.
3. Being able to plan and manage one's time effectively.
4. Being able to create the enthusiasm and motivation to follow through ideas.

Getting people to view new ideas favourably when they are not disposed to do so is essentially one of changing attitudes. In order to do this they must, in the first place, become dissatisfied with the status quo. People do not readily recognize that they *are* dissatisfied; thus, the first task may be to show them this. This can be achieved in several different ways:

(a) Create an awareness of problems that actually exist and get people to recognize that there is a need to change and adopt the idea that is being put forward.
(b) Warn people about the potential hazards of not accepting change.
(c) Stress the benefits of change to the individuals concerned, as they will only be motivated to adopt new ideas when they perceive that it is in their own best interest to do so.

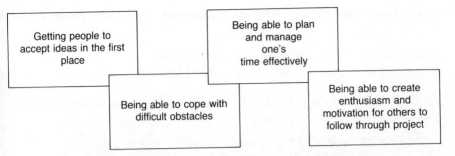

Figure 11.3 Conditions necessary to get ideas implemented.

There is obviously much to be gained from blending all three approaches when trying to get a new idea accepted.

Communication theories propose several descriptive models of the process by which people adopt ideas as a result of receiving information about them. The models can also be used prescriptively as aids to producing communication messages that bring about action.

The first of these models, the AIDA model, variously described, argues that there are four stages which a communicator has to put into effect when trying to bring about action in someone:

☐ attracting *attention*;

☐ maintaining *interest*;

☐ arousing *desire*; and

☐ getting *action*.

People, it is argued, move through these stages in a logical order and the communicator has to help move people through these stages. The model is commonly used by sales people when holding a sales interview.

In 1961, Lavidge and Steiner developed the 'hierarchy of effects' model. This model contained many of the ideas discussed above and was directly related to advertising. The model, presented below, suggests a 6-stage process through which the person moves:

AWARENESS → KNOWLEDGE → LIKING → PREFERENCE → CONVICTION → PURCHASE

In the same year, Colley (1961) produced a model called DAGMAR, which stands for defining advertising goals, measuring advertising results. It argued that a communication must carry a prospect through four levels of understanding:

AWARENESS → COMPREHENSION → CONVICTION → ACTION

In the following year the 'innovation adoption' model was published by Rogers (1962).

$$\text{AWARENESS} \to \text{INTEREST} \to \text{EVALUATION} \to$$
$$\text{TRIAL} \to \text{ADOPTION}$$

All these models seem to fit in well with the more general communications model of:

$$\text{EXPOSURE} \to \text{RECEPTION} \to \text{COGNITIVE RESPONSE} \to$$
$$\text{ATTITUDE} \to \text{INTENTION} \to \text{BEHAVIOUR}$$

This general model of communication suggests that people have to be exposed to a message and receive it. The cognitive response stage refers to becoming aware and informed about the subject of the message – awareness and comprehension. The attitude stage corresponds to the development of a liking, interest, desire or preference. Intention simply precedes actual behaviour and corresponds with conviction or trial.

The main point about all these models is that attitude change is seen as a step-by-step process and not one that can necessarily be implemented with great speed. The above models will be appropriate for different circumstances depending upon exactly what is required with respect to the idea that has to be implemented.

Reducing resistance to change

Getting people to change their attitudes is the heart of reducing resistance to change. Creating dissatisfaction with the status quo is one method of effecting attitude change and getting new ideas implemented. However, there are also a number of other ways of achieving the same goal.

In the first place, one has to accept that resistance to change is quite a normal response. People are apt to find change threatening because they are afraid that it will in some way have a negative effect upon them. For example, where a team of workers have been performing a task in a certain way for a considerable length of time and where they are paid according to what they produce they will naturally fear both for their income, or lack of it, and even for their jobs if a new method is suggested. It is a good policy to meet resistance to change with openness and honesty. At the end of the day, if it is intended to introduce change there is no point in not disclosing the fact. Open and honest communication is a powerful remedy to the threat of uncertainty.

A good way to counter resistance to change is to pre-empt the possibility of it occurring. Getting people involved in the idea development process and taking note of their ideas in the first place anticipates resistance to change. Resistance is reduced because people feel that they have had the opportunity to participate and express their view.

In the same way that the initial attitude change itself has to be seen as a gradual process, the implementation of large changes should follow a similar pattern. New ideas that involve substantial change need to be implemented gradually, smoothly and systematically.

Resistance to change can be softened by making the changes tentative rather than definite or permanent. It is a good strategy to get people to try out ideas initially for a short period. People should be encouraged to give feedback as to whether they think the idea is working. If a new idea fails it does not cause its originator as much loss of face under such circumstances.

Encouraging people to recognize that change is a normal facet of life is important. If they come to accept this they will not see it as being out of the ordinary when it is applied to them. It can help them to become less emotionally attached to the status quo.

One has to be reasonably sure that the change is worthwhile. Change does have a cost, not the least part of which is the disruption it causes to those concerned. Provided that the change brings with it demonstrable benefits which more than offset the costs of disruption, the change is more likely to meet with little resistance. Moreover, it paves the way for the introduction of future change in that it is more likely to be seen in the interest of the organization.

Coping with criticism

Anyone who tries to effect change will meet with his or her fair share of criticism. After all, being critical of a suggested or impending change is a natural defence mechanism to be aired by those who are resistant to the change.

People naturally dislike criticism and are apt to take it as a personal attack on themselves. The important thing to bear in mind, however, is that it is not the criticism that is unpleasant, but people's reaction to the criticism. Once this is recognized one is a long way down the road to being able to deal with criticism. Often the criticism is ill-founded and even if this is not the case we can usually benefit from the views expressed by others – even if it is too late to do anything about it on this occasion we can bear it in mind for the future.

Consensus mapping

Consensus mapping helps participants to visualize, analyze and organize ideas that are interrelated and sequence dependent. It involves creating

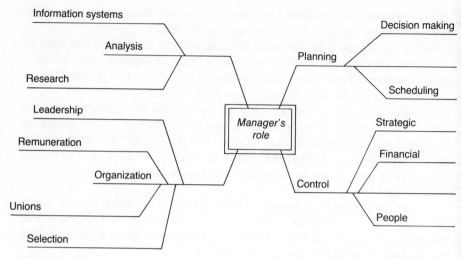

Figure 11.4   Mind-mapping techniques, drawn using InfoMap Lite (see p. 215).

a graphic map that shows clusters of ideas and indicates how they are presumed to be interrelated (Figure 11.4).

The map becomes modified as participants discuss it. The final map is then used as an implementation guide. The steps involved are discussed briefly below.

Looking for a structure
First, individuals try to identify clusters and categories for grouping the ideas. This is done initially on an individual basis and then groups prepare their own classification schemes based on individual contributions.

Development of an initial map
The ideas of the various groups are next consolidated into one map. This is then presented to all groups for discussion.

Map reconfiguration
The groups study the initial map and make use of it as a stimulus for developing solution maps of their own. These are produced by writing ideas on Post-It™ notes and placing the notes on sheets of newsprint or similar material. The notes can then be shifted around from one position to another and modified as desired. Ribbon or string can be used to show a relationship or flow of information and activities between positions on the map.

Presentation to the whole group
Groups eventually reconvene and compare maps offering comments and querying each others' maps.

Map consolidation

Finally, representatives from each group convene to produce a single map that incorporates features from them all.

Potential problem analysis

Kepner and Tregoe (1976) developed this method to prevent problems from occurring during implementation and to reduce their effects should they occur. The steps involved in the process are as follows:

1. The first step is to work out exactly what should take place if the solution or idea to be implemented is to be done so successfully. Where what should happen does not materialize, this would be seen as a potential problem.
2. Reverse brainstorming is then employed to identify everything that could go wrong once a solution has been implemented. This will generate a list of potential problems.
3. With respect to each identified potential problem the specific nature of each potential problem that has been identified is highlighted in detail.
4. The critical nature of each of the identified potential problems, in terms of its impact on the success or failure of the whole project, is then judged and evaluated. Sources of problems which appear to have a critical impact on a project will require extra monitoring during implementation and must be dealt with effectively should they arise.
5. Judgement and previous experience are used to search for and identify possible causes of each problem.
6. The probability of occurrence of the potential causes is determined, again using judgement and experience.
7. Ways of preventing the causes and minimizing their effect in the event that they do arise are worked out.
8. Contingency plans for the most serious problems are developed.

Example
A new sales force is to be recruited and trained to provide a new approach to marketing directly to retailing outlets.

What should happen?
Nine sales people need to be recruited within the next 3 months. All should complete a 3-day training programme at the company's staff training centre prior to receiving on-the-job instruction from the sales manager over the

subsequent 6 weeks. The 3-day training programme is to be mounted jointly by the sales manager and other senior staff of the company in conjunction with a consultancy firm specializing in sales training.

Everything that possibly can go wrong – potential problems

(a) Failure to recruit nine sales staff.

(b) Recruits not of a sufficient calibre for training.

(c) Training company unable to help put on course.

(d) Quality of input by training company below what is expected.

(e) Sales staff leave before completion of training programme.

(f) Company staff unable to attend course.

(g) Inputs from company staff below what is expected.

(h) Sales manager unable to give on-the-job training.

(i) Not all the new sales staff are able to start at the same time.

Specific nature of the problem

(a) The supply of good quality sales staff is poor and it may not be possible to get nine such sales people.

(b) It may not be possible to start all new sales staff on the same day, week or even month. This will clearly make it difficult or impossible to run the 3-day training programme as planned.

Critical impact of the problems on the sales training programme

Items (a) and (b) will have a critical impact on the project. Poor quality or insufficient numbers of recruits will affect the viability of the project. All the other identified problems clearly have a substantial impact on the project.

Possible cause of each problem

(a) Failure to recruit nine sales staff – insufficient supply.

(b) Recruits not of a sufficient calibre for training – insufficient supply.

(c) Training company unable to help put on course – unforeseen circumstances.

(d) Quality of input by training company below what is expected – consultants' quality of service unknown beforehand.

(e) Sales staff leave before completion of training programme – find other, more desirable, employment.

(f) Company staff unable to attend course – illness.

(g) Inputs from company staff below what is expected – lack of experience.

(h) Sales manager unable to give on-the-job training – too many other commitments.

(i) Not all the new sales staff are able to start at the same time – people have to work out different notices when terminating their current jobs.

Establish the probability of occurrence of the potential causes, again using judgement and experience

Develop ways of preventing the causes and minimizing their effect in the event that they do in fact arise

(a) Failure to recruit nine sales staff – put a lot of effort into recruitment, use recruitment agency.

(b) Recruits not of a sufficient calibre for training – as in (a).

(c) Training company unable to help put on course – choose reliable consultants with a good track record.

(d) Quality of input by training company below what is expected – as in (c).

(e) Sales staff leave before completion of training programme to find other more desirable employment – provide them with a good incentive to stay.

(f) Company staff unable to attend course – have people who can stand in if required.

(g) Inputs from company staff below what is expected – pick people who are most likely to make good contributions.

(h) Sales manager unable to give on-the-job training – reschedule or delegate work.

(i) Not all the new sales staff are able to start at the same time – run more than one 3-day training programme.

Develop contingency plans for the most serious problems

(a) Failure to recruit nine sales staff – plan to manage with less sales staff.

(b) Recruits not of a sufficient calibre for training – as in (a).

(c) Training company unable to help put on course – have a back-up firm who is able to help out at short notice.

(d) Quality of input by training company below what is expected – make sure own staff can compensate for any serious inadequacies.

(e) Sales staff leave before completion of training programme – keep file of potential recruits 'live'.

(f) Company staff unable to attend course – have stand-ins available.

(g) Inputs from company staff below what is expected – as in (f).

(h) Sales manager unable to give on-the-job training – hire specialist on-the-job trainer.

(i) Not all the new sales staff are able to start at the same time – run more than one 3-day training course.

Research planning diagrams

Getting ideas implemented has much to do with systematic planning. In reality many managers use a variety of methods to assist in planning and controlling work activities. The variety of techniques used can vary considerably in terms of sophistication and complexity. At one extreme they may involve the construction of PERT networks while at the other extreme they may comprise simple flowcharts.

Between the two extremes of methods there are what are known as Research Planning Diagrams (RPD) (see Van Gundy, 1988). An RPD is constructed using logic borrowed from computer flow diagrams. Rectangular boxes indicate actions and diamond-shaped boxes indicate decision points. The procedure for using RPDs is as follows:

1. The objectives should be stated and it should be quite clear what end result is expected.

2. The actions required to implement the idea should be listed, commencing with the first required activity and then listing the remaining activities in the required sequence.

3. For every activity, the important questions that must be satisfied *before* succeeding activities can take place should be listed. These questions then function as the decision points in the subsequent diagram.

4. The diagram is constructed using the information generated above. Arrows are used to connect activities and decision points and thereby indicate the flow of action throughout the diagram. If it is appropriate, time estimates and probabilities can be assigned to decision points in due course.

5. Where a response to a decision point is difficult to determine a 'rethink' response should be indicated.

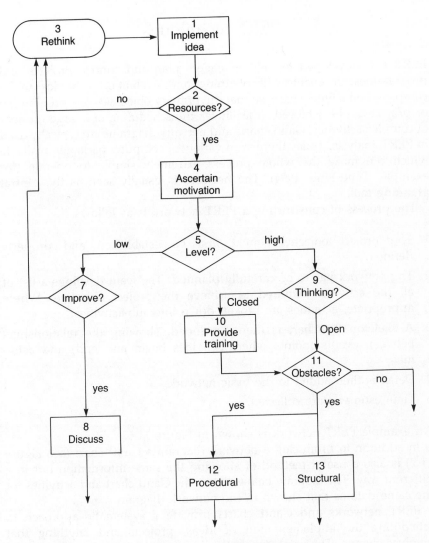

Figure 11.5 RPD diagram.

An example of a partially completed diagram is shown in Figure 11.5. The diagram shows that in line with the above text one first ascertains whether sufficient resources are available (or can be obtained) to enable implementation of the project to take place. Next, one considers levels of motivation and whether these can be provided for. Closed thinking is seen as something for which training can be given if it is required. Boxes 12 and 13 indicate the presence of procedural and structural blocks.

PERT techniques

PERT was developed to help managers plan and control projects and programmes. It enables all planning and evaluation activities to be completed on a timely basis so that the primary objectives of a programme or project can be achieved. It facilitates the scheduling of a large number of complex activities. Gantt charts and network diagrams are typically used in PERT analysis. Today there are a variety of computer packages available which can make the whole process extremely simple to operate (for example, Time Line, 1994). The network is usually seen as the central planning tool.

The process of constructing a PERT network is as follows.

1. The project objectives must first be established and properly defined.

2. The network has to be carefully planned. The team develops a list of all the activities required to achieve the project objective. Where appropriate, activities are broken down into sub-activities.

3. A skeleton flowchart is then developed, showing the relationships between events (points where activities begin and end) and activities.

4. Detail is then added to the basic network.

5. Time estimates are collected.

An example PERT network is shown in Figure 11.6.

In addition to producing a network diagram a Gantt chart (see Figure 11.7) is also a useful method of showing the same information but in a different way. The diagram below shows the Gantt chart and activities for the same data as that shown in the network diagram.

PERT networks and Gantt charts provide a systematic approach to scheduling the implementation of ideas, projects and anything that involves change. They also enable those concerned to see exactly what is involved and when it will affect them. Seeing the whole project in perspective helps to understand what is happening or about to happen.

Computerized PERT networks have the added advantage in that they allow for changes in schedules to be calculated very quickly and for their effect on the overall project to be rapidly assessed. They also allow simulated projects to be evaluated since one can vary the amount of time activities take and the order in which they occur. Activities may also be included or excluded from the analysis.

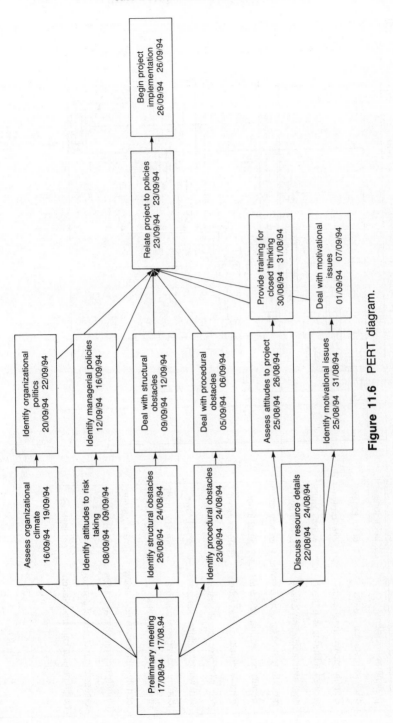

Figure 11.6 PERT diagram.

Figure 11.7 Gantt chart.

Post implementation

Getting one's ideas put into practice is comparable to selling a technical product to an industrial user. The job is not over when the sale is clinched or the idea actually put into practice. As in the case of selling the product, one has to make sure that what was implemented actually works for more than a couple of days and does not fall down because of some oversight which has not been foreseen. That is not to say that there will not be complaints about what has been implemented. It is quite likely that the problem solver(s) will be inundated with messages from both people who supported and opposed the new idea to the effect that the new idea does not seem to be working properly.

Receiving messages, usually complaints, is to be expected. Indeed, it would be quite unusual if complaints were not generated. As long as one realizes that complaints are to be expected then one can cope more easily with the kind of problems that do arise. Usually there are three types of message about any new idea that has been implemented:

(a) *Grousing* – these usually do not call for action and simply reflect people's resistance to change. They will complain simply because they are required to do things in a different way.

(b) *Errors of detail* – even the most carefully thought-out ideas often overlook aspects of detail. When the element of detail is not critical it is usually possible to 'think on one's feet' and modify the implementation so that it covers whatever is required. Elements that are critical to the functioning of the whole, however, are more problematic and may call for some quick thinking. In some cases they may even temporarily hold up matters until they can be sorted out.

(c) *Apparently major errors* – these can be either real or supposed. In the latter case it is simply a matter of reassuring management that it is only supposition. Where they are real then a whole project or programme may crash as a result. Under the latter circumstances the implementer of the idea has more than his or her reputation to think of.

What the above goes to show is that ideas must be workable and reliable. Thinking through and testing out ideas before they are finally implemented is highlighted as a critical stage of the process.

References

Colley, R. H. (1961) *Defining Advertising Goals for Measuring Advertising Effectiveness*, New York: Association of National Advertising.

Hart, S., Boroush, M., Enk, G. and Hornick, W. (1985) 'Managing complexity through consensus mapping: technology for the managing of group decisions', *Academy of Management Review*, **10**(3), 587–600.

Kepner, C. H. and Tregoe, B. B. (1976) *The Rational Manager*, Princeton, NJ: Kepner-Tregoe.

Lavidge, R. J. and Steiner, G. A. (1961) 'A model for predictive measurements of advertising effectiveness', *Journal of Marketing*, **25**, October, 59–62.

Rogers, E. (1962) *Diffusion of Innovations*, New York: Free Press of Glencoe.

Time Line (1994) Project management software published by Symantec, Cupertino, California.

Van Gundy, A. B. (1988) *Techniques of Structured Problem Solving*, New York: Van Nostrand Reinhold.

12

Computer assisted creativity

Simon (1985) discussed a computer program called BACON, which he had developed with co-workers. He contended that if a computer program was able to make discoveries which, if made by a human, could be deemed creative, then the processes it used should provide useful information about the creative process. The BACON program received raw observational or experimental data and produced, when successful, scientific laws. Simon wanted to show that scientific discovery is an understandable phenomenon which can be explained in terms of all the same kinds of basic information processes that account for other kinds of human problem solving and thinking. Simon's efforts were directed at getting a computer to undertake creative problem solving by itself.

In contrast to Simon's approach, other researchers have looked at the interaction between people and machines as a means of producing creative problem solving. Early attempts at producing computer assisted problem-solving aids were made in the late 1970s and coincided with the advent of the microcomputer. The methods employed had a theoretical basis in the work of Rogers (1954), Maslow (1954) and Kelly (1955). Rogers and Maslow supported the view that self-discovery might improve creativity while Kelly argued that the loosening of constructs led to the gaining of creative insights. Rokeach (1979) devised a computer program which enabled individuals to examine their own value systems. Rokeach's work illustrated the potential effects that a computer program could have for clarifying the user's own knowledge. A more complex knowledge clarification program, PLANET, designed by Mildred Shaw (1982), helped the user to discover the themes and variations in his or her own individual problems. A key feature of the program was the Repertory Grid (Kelly, 1955), and it was this that helped comprehension of the classifications people constructed around their experiences and, if required, to reconstruct views on a problem.

Role of computers in creativity

One does not typically associate computers with an organization's search for new ideas and creative problem solving. They are more usually associated with improving efficiency in routine decision making. However, there are ways in which computers can assist the creative process. These can take relatively unstructured or highly structured forms (see Young, 1989) (Figure 12.1). To be useful, however, it is argued that the computer assisted techniques should:

☐ provide a structuring mechanism for solving a problem along with appropriate means of stimulating creative thinking, generated by the computer program; or

☐ facilitate/improve the mechanisms of conventional techniques.

In evaluating the software discussed below I will consider whether the different softwares help in any of these respects.

Computer aided creativity can offer advantages over non-computer assisted methods. The advantages differ according to whether one is considering group creative problem solving or individual creative problem solving. In the case of group creative problem solving it is essential that they facilitate creative problem solving for members of a group who are separated physically from one another by distance. That is, the individuals may be in different buildings or even in different towns. In the case of individual creative problem solving the advantage lies in the structuring mechanism that the programs provide for the user and, in some cases, a stimulus to thought in the absence of other people.

According to Young (1989) creativity decision support systems are evolving rapidly. He envisages them as automating creativity tools such as morphological analysis and brainstorming. The prime objective of creativity support systems should be to facilitate both convergent and divergent thinking processes.

However, the fundamental design of creativity support systems should be such that they facilitate both convergent and divergent thinking processes. They also need to incorporate domain-specific knowledge to facilitate each of these two phases of creative thinking. In addition, as shown in Figure 12.1, they also need to facilitate the process of creative problem solving.

1. Does the package facilitate movement through any or all of the stages of creative problem solving? i.e. problem definition, idea generation, idea evaluation

2. Does the package provide any mechanisms which stimulate thought? i.e. metaphors, random words, etc.

3. Does the package provide a structuring framework within which to define problems, generate ideas or evaluate ideas?

4. Does the package facilitate or improve the use of conventional creative problem-solving aids?

Figure 12.1 Criteria for evaluating computer software which aids creative problem solving.

Computer assisted idea generation for individuals

Most of the computer assisted mechanisms discussed in this section are intended primarily for use by individuals. However, all of them can, of course, be used in a group situation – provided that all members of the group are present. First we will look at computer software that is not specifically designed for helping the creative problem solving process but which can be used for the purpose.

Electronic mail

An electronic mail system provides an illustration of how a relatively unstructured mechanism can aid the creative thinking process in business. It facilitates the informal exchange of ideas.

'Groupware' has developed out of the use of electronic mail systems in this way, and is the name given to computer software that enables people to swap ideas and other information at a distance. Several software houses offer groupware packages and among those available is Lotus Notes™. The information can take the form of notes, spreadsheets, graphics or images.

Spreadsheets

Spreadsheets themselves may facilitate the creative thinking process. They do this by allowing the user to construct simple or complex mathematical models which make it easy to try out sensitivity analysis. This is both a powerful and a simple way of encouraging creative thinking. It encourages

Initial scenario

		1st Q	2nd Q	3rd Q	4th Q	Total
Revenue		£6,516	£6,516	£6,516	£6,516	£26,064
Cost of goods	75%	£4,887	£4,887	£4,887	£4,887	£19,548
Gross contribution		£1,629	£1,629	£1,629	£1,629	£6,516
Advertising expense		£200	£200	£200	£200	£800
Net contribution		£1,429	£1,429	£1,429	£1,429	£5,716

Second scenario

		1st Q	2nd Q	3rd Q	4th Q	Total
Revenue		£6,516	£6,516	£6,516	£6,516	£26,064
Cost of goods	65%	£4,235	£4,235	£4,235	£4,235	£16,942
Gross contribution		£2,281	£2,281	£2,281	£2,281	£9,122
Advertising expense		£200	£200	£200	£200	£800
Net contribution		£2,081	£2,081	£2,081	£2,081	£8,322

Third scenario

		1st Q	2nd Q	3rd Q	4th Q	Total
Revenue		£6,516	£6,516	£6,516	£6,516	£26,064
Cost of goods	65%	£4,235	£4,235	£4,235	£4,235	£16,942
Gross contribution		£2,281	£2,281	£2,281	£2,281	£9,122
Advertising expense		£100	£300	£500	£300	£1,200
Net contribution		£2,181	£1,981	£1,781	£1,981	£7,922

Figure 12.2 Sensitivity analysis with a spreadsheet.

people to try out ideas in a risk-free environment and provides a ready-made tool for doing so.

Spreadsheets permit the construction of quite sophisticated models and one can, for example, examine the effect of changing the cost of goods sold and advertising on overall net contribution (see Figure 12.2).

Simulation packages

Even more sophisticated than spreadsheets are simulation packages that enable one to try out ideas through computer simulation rather than in reality in the first instance. Microcomputers and associated software have brought the power of management science techniques and models to the fingertips of the management services expert. The application of powerful techniques to real problems can have substantial pay-offs in helping to uncover satisfactory solutions to difficult problems.

Complex situations can be modelled with the aid of such software as Powersim and MicroSaint which run in a Windows environment. Such packages as these allow discrete event modelling and task networks. They enable the user to build models which simulate real-life processes. Common application areas for the packages include:

□ modelling manufacturing processes, such as production lines, to examine issues such as resource utilization, efficiency and cost;

□ modelling transportation systems to examine issues such as scheduling and resource requirements;

□ modelling human services systems to optimize procedures, staffing and other logistical considerations;

□ modelling training systems and their effectiveness over time; and

□ modelling human operator performance and interaction under changing conditions.

The packages permit the user to model any process that can be represented in a flowchart diagram, as a network of tasks (see below). The model can include dynamically changing variables, probabilistic and tactical branching logic, sorted queues, conditional task execution and extensive data collection. The programs symbolically animate the network diagrams as they execute the model and, after running the model, one can obtain statistics, charts and graphs to analyze collected data.

Figure 12.3 shows a still of the animated flowchart for a simulation of people entering and using a dining facility. It shows them entering the dining hall, being served a variety of foods and drink, taking their places at a table, eating their meals and then departing in due course. Individuals are shown as symbols in the diagram (squares, circles, triangles) and one can see from the diagram how bottlenecks or queues occur at various serving points, for example.

Databases

The manipulation and searching of databases present a relatively unstructured approach to creative problem solving. Internal records can be scanned to help solve customers' problems. External databases can be searched for information that has an influence on pending organizational decisions. Marketing databases can supply the means to identify target customers and in this context database marketing is now a well established *modus operandi*. Moreover, database searching has been used to search for new product ideas (Bar, 1989).

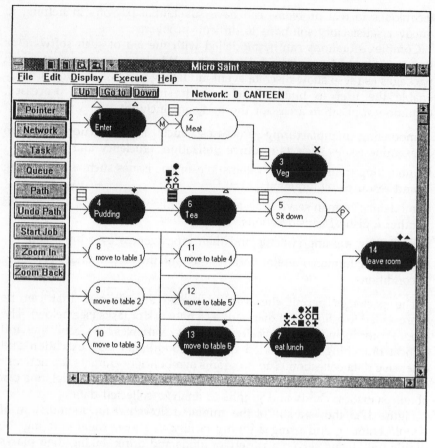

Figure 12.3 Animated flowchart using MicroSaint.

Computer aided design

In addition to general applications software of the kind discussed above, more specialized software is available for individuals who are involved in design and modelling. The use of such software speeds up the design and modelling processes involved.

Special purpose software

There are also applications of information technology which have been expressly designed to assist in the generation of solutions to open-ended problems. At the simplest level they comprise programs which assist with the capture and restructuring of unstructured thoughts. More complex software has been developed that simulates well-known and tried creative problem-solving aids such as brainstorming and morphological analysis (for example, see Young 1989). Some of these kinds of packages are discussed next.

Restructuring thoughts

Ideas organization packages permit people to record their own ideas, as they occur, for subsequent review. Brainstorm is an example of such a package. The user can key in a list of ideas relating to a specific topic. Further ideas can be added to the list or ideas already entered can be expanded at a subsequent time. The product of the interaction is a 'brainstorm model' and the user can restructure this at will and in such a way that it provides insights into a problem. It is also possible to merge models so that individuals working on the same problem can produce a consolidated model if they so wish.

InfoMap Lite is a productivity tool for Windows that brings the power of mind maps® to the graphical PC environment. Introduced in the 1970s by Tony Buzan, the mind map has become widespread in its use for brainstorming, idea creation, document planning and note taking.

A mind map is a simple system of organizing and visualizing information in a predominantly hierarchical manner, whereby information is attached to branches radiating from the map centre and hierarchical relationships are visualized by branches attached as the 'children' of others. Non-hierarchical relationships are supported in InfoMap Lite by map links embedded in the maps.

Mind maps have myriad uses and are already used extensively in project management and time management, and are becoming an increasingly popular tool in educational (both professional and academic) contexts. Here are some of the things for which mind maps can be used:

☐ structuring to-do lists and action plans;

☐ planning and recording meetings;

☐ problem solving and 'brainstorming';

☐ document structuring ('outlining');

☐ making effective presentations; and

☐ reducing and handling complexity.

In translating the concept of mind maps to the graphical PC environment InfoMap Lite not only capitalizes on the mind map's ease of use and ease

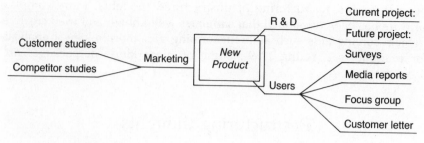

Figure 12.4 Part of a 'mind map' from InfoMap Lite.

of learning (Figure 12.4), but adds a number of significant advantages over the manually produced variety:

☐ It provides an efficient, organized method of textual data-entry (especially useful, for example, for taking and organizing notes in a meeting).

☐ The mind map's layout is automatically changed to reflect its changing topology, making room for new branches as they are added (no more squeezing new branches into a small corner of the page!), or closing up gaps left by deleted branches.

☐ Maps can be easily rearranged (move or copy a section of a map simply by dragging it to a new location in the same, or to a different, map), making them a flexible tool for experimenting with different ideas or information relationships.

☐ The view of a displayed or printed map can be altered to highlight particular sub-trees within the map or expanded and collapsed in an 'outline' fashion to hide or expose detail.

☐ By the attachment of display styles to parts of a mind map, items of information or other arbitrary relationships between them can be highlighted visually through the use of colour and fount styles.

Brainbox is another program which enables one to construct 'thought maps'. It provides mappers with a set of process-based tools based on the mapping technique known as concept sorting. Manual methods of concept sorting involve, first, writing ideas on small squares of paper and then sorting these into clusters. The clusters of paper squares are stuck down on a large sheet of paper and lines drawn between ideas or clusters of ideas to emphasize the more important relationships. Brainbox enhances this technique by enabling the user to perform the task on a computer.

Another package which enables one to link and restructure one's own ideas is WEB. WEB is a hypertext application in which text is arranged

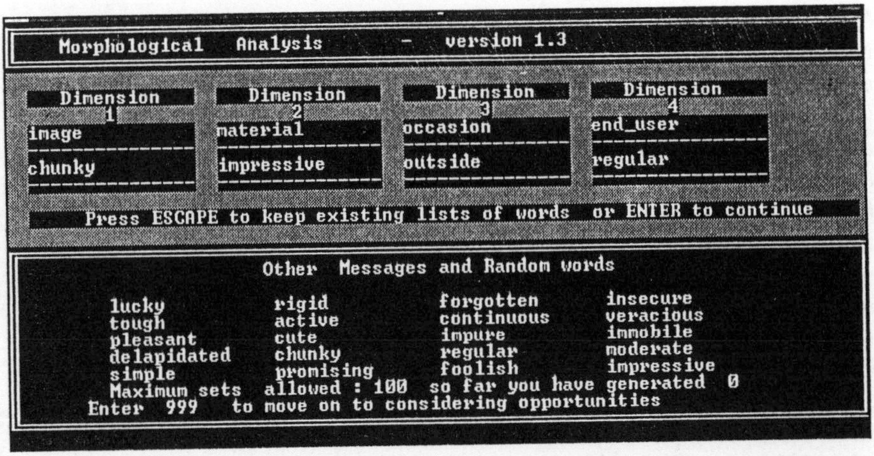

Figure 12.5 Entering attributes for identified dimensions in MORPHY.

in what are called 'frames'. A frame can be a sentence, paragraph or list, relating to a single item of information. Frames are linked together by threads. A thread is a number of related frames, arranged in an order to suit the user. The user can mix and match frames to form new threads. As with Brainstorm, information and ideas can be recorded in an *ad hoc* fashion.

Creative problem-solving techniques emulators

Morphological analysis
Some software emulates well-known creative problem-solving aids. Morphological analysis involves generating many combinations of attributes which have then to be examined and evaluated. Managing and sorting the often large number of combinations in order to identify potential winners can be a considerable task. MORPHY (Proctor, 1989) is a software product which has been developed to do exactly this. MORPHY prompts the user to enter the dimensions of the product under consideration and to list the attributes (see Figure 12.5). Furthermore, it builds on the basic model of morphological analysis by providing the user with suggestions for possible attributes by means of randomly generated adjectives, which the user may select or ignore. All the possible combinations of a user-defined subset can be rapidly recalled and reviewed. From these the user can then select those that should be stored for further analysis.

Synectics

MindLink Problem Solver is based on major synectics principles and concepts. In particular it employs 'triggers' to stimulate ideas. Triggers force together a concept or thought apparently unrelated to a problem and attempt to arouse ideas through such combinations. The Solution Machine also employs the synectics approach to creative problem solving. Among the techniques employed is the presentation of an imaginary situation such as 'a musical robot analysing a house with a piece of string'. The users of the program have then to visualize the imaginary situation and describe it in detail. Next, the users have to use the situation descriptions as stimuli to generate ideas with respect to the real problem on which they are working.

Lateral thinking and synectics programs are not in plentiful supply. The Idea Generator Plus encourages deferment of judgement and uses a variety of techniques to help generate ideas. These include: considering similar situations, examining metaphors, thinking of how someone else might solve the problem, reversing the problem, and transforming ideas which were previously considered inappropriate.

Other methods

A different kind of software altogether facilitates thought provocation. IdeaFisher from Idea Systems Inc. of Irvine, California, United States, is designed to assist idea generation. The program enables one to follow the strand of an idea through its Idea Bank, a 7-megabyte database of words and phrases. In essence any initial word starts the user on a trail of thousands of related objects and concepts which are intended to arouse creative thinking. It includes a rich dictionary ranging from existentialism to ear-wax, Archimedes to Al Capone and Pan-Slavism to padded toilet seats and there are more than 65 000 entries. Choosing a subject calls up various tangible or symbolic images for the user to develop. The principal way of using the package is to choose a word and browse through the database using the electronic notepad provided to record ideas gained in the process.

There is also a databank of some 3000 questions which is used afterwards to 'talk you through' an idea. The questions are assembled according to purpose, and prompt the user to refine a selected topic. Responding to whatever the user enters, the package generates a list of words and phrases and presents them to the user. These are referred to as 'key concepts'. The user can make use of these key concepts as a base for searching for related associations. IdeaFisher facilitates the retrieving and restructuring of existing groups of ideas into new ideas.

Following this the program filters the user's answers to specify key concepts which can then be re-presented to the Idea Bank for further analysis. The development of the software is said to have cost millions of dollars and 12 years of research.

IdeaFisher provides the user with that all-important stimulus to think creatively and does not simply act as a structuring mechanism for recording one's own thoughts. Much of the previously developed software failed to meet this important criterion.

The number of computer assisted idea-generating aids for individuals has increased over the years. In Table 12.1 a sample list and brief description of the kinds of program that have been developed are presented.

The good points of many of these programs, however, are largely confined to idea generation rather than with respect to problem definition and evaluation of ideas. Moreover, the lack of stimuli to help people think creatively, other than that provided by the structuring of the process itself, which is present in some of these programs, does little to enhance the creative problem-solving process.

Group creative problem-solving aids

Aids to creative problem solving include group techniques as well as techniques for individuals. The merging of perspectives and views has in the past been found to be a productive way of discovering new insights into stubborn problems.

Group aids to creative thinking have also been emulated by computer decision support mechanisms. In addition to facilities for individuals, networked personal computers provide the surroundings for software which can assemble and amalgamate the ideas of different individuals. A team can use an application to evaluate and rank ideas which have either been generated in a group brainstorming session or are the result of individual efforts collated on the network. This kind of software saves time and permits equality of opportunity to input ideas. It also facilitates the gaining of a consensus of opinion.

There are two main products on the market in the United States that can be used for this purpose. TeamFocus, developed by the University of Arizona, and VisionQuest, developed by Collaborative Technologies Corporation of Austin, Texas. TeamFocus can be used by a group of individuals who meet electronically on their decision network. Participants can work from any location provided that they have suitable computer hardware. An alternative is for individuals to work on their own and network their ideas later.

Robert L. A. Trost at the Centre for Commercial Innovation Ltd in the Netherlands has produced 'Global Think Tank'. This package makes use

Table 12.1 Some computerized creativity aids, and their main features

Computerized creativity aid	Features
Cope (1980)	☐ Facilitates the construction of cognitive maps. Useful for gaining insights into one's own beliefs and attitudes with respect to a problem. Helps to identify potential blocks to implementing new ideas
BRIAN (1985)	☐ Helps to structure problems and make decisions. Includes a module which performs morphological analysis. Useful for generating new product ideas
BRAIN (1985)	☐ Helps to define open-ended problems and to stimulate insights. Uses random words and semi-meaningful phrases. Useful in identifying new ways to do something
Idea Generator (1986)	☐ Useful for structuring problems. Includes a framework for generating insights by analogy
Idea Tree (1988)	☐ A computerized tool that facilitates mind-mapping. It is good for obtaining insights into how a problem is structured
MORPHY (1989)	☐ A package facilitating morphological analysis and including a random word generator to aid identification of attributes. Useful for generating new product ideas, etc.
IdeaFisher (1990)	☐ Uses word association to enable one to follow through the thread of an idea
Thunder Thought (1990)	☐ Essentially a random word generator to help the stimulation of insights. This can be achieved by 'force-fitting' a randomly generated phrase with the problem in hand. See Figure 12.6, where the program has produced a list of 'images'
MoonLite (1993)	☐ Assists in dreaming up creative ideas. MoonLite is based on the premise that at least 80 per cent of one's tangible and intangible assets are not being fully used and are, in fact, more or less lying idle. In order to activate this potential, MoonLite employs a new creativity technique called Random Asset Pairing (RAP) with which tangible and intangible assets that you have or can dispose of are randomly combined and presented in ever-changing pairs to form the basis for the pleasant and easy generation of creative business ideas. Enables one to work through objective setting, idea generating and evaluation (see Figure 12.7).
BizIdea	☐ The commercial version of BizIdea is a more advanced program than MoonLite, making use of Fuzzy Logic in the determination and rating of criteria.

```
┌─────────────────────────────────────────────┐
│                    IMAGES                     │
│                 brainy triplets               │
│             irregularly hesitate coda         │
│               sweet translations              │
│            privately ponder message           │
│                worthless motions              │
│            disgracefully claim couplet        │
│           superficial individualities         │
│              helpfully discuss act            │
│               intense submissions             │
│           deliberately study artistry         │
│                  sincere tales                │
│               never struggle meter            │
│               foolish manuscripts             │
│                  listen fiction               │
│             intellectual publishers           │
│           professionally fondle coda          │
│                dishonest interests            │
│             suspiciously laugh pen            │
│                 repulsive presses             │
│            quickly eliminate science          │
│           PRESS ⟨ENTER⟩ TO CONTINUE           │
└─────────────────────────────────────────────┘
```

Figure 12.6 Images from Thunder Thought.

of a program called Operation Brainstorm. The package facilitates idea generation and can be used over electronic networks such as CompuServe or Internet. The Operation Brainstorm program produces a workfile in which the output of a brainstorming session is filed. The workfile can be exchanged with another person using a disk or electronic file – no matter where the person lives.

Both these packages improve productivity through the medium of computerized group decision making. They aim to reduce executives' time spent in meetings and enhance creativity. Electronic group brainstorming sessions are anonymous, thus removing an important barrier to creative thinking – the fear of feeling foolish in front of superiors. The elimination of social inhibitions can lead to the generation of novel and unusual ideas.

OptionFinder is another package which can be used by a group. It is readily available in the United Kingdom and is designed to provoke thought and explore the different opinions held by the people who might use it. The system consists of a public screen and a single personal computer loaded with the software. The system is portable and is used to facilitate voting on issues identified by a facilitator. Voting is anonymous but comment is not. Voting analysis is displayed in a graphical format,

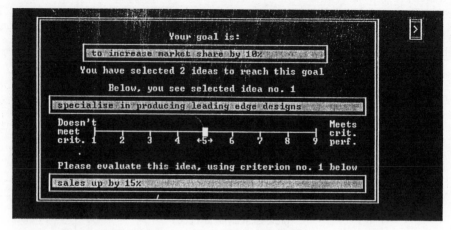

Figure 12.7   Evaluating ideas against criteria using MoonLite.

either on an x–y grid or as a bar chart on the public screen. This analysis of opinion enhances evaluation and feedback. It clarifies whether there is consensus of opinion or disagreement. Confirmation of conflicting beliefs can induce thought-provoking exchanges and new ideas.

Evaluation of the alternatives

There are different ways of evaluating alternative options. A rating scale, whereby alternatives are ranked against a full set of criteria, provides the simplest method. This can be constructed easily with the aid of a Lotus 123™ spreadsheet, or any other spreadsheet. UDECIDE, produced by Cascoly Software, offers a user-friendly approach to rating alternatives against criteria and may be preferred to the spreadsheet approach.

Implementation of ideas

Both Kelly (1955) and Rogers (1954) underlined the importance of understanding one's own cognitive processes as an integral component of the creative process. Gaining such an understanding can be greatly helped through the use of 'mind-mapping' techniques.

A cognitive map is a network of ideas and is illustrated as nodes linked by arrows, representing goals and actions. SODA (Strategic Option Development Analysis) is such a methodology and uses a computer model

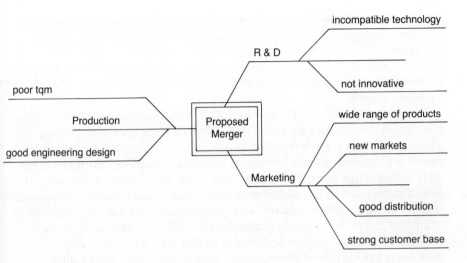

Figure 12.8 Use of mapping tool to show views of different departments about a proposed merger.

called COPE to help in the analysis. A facilitator interviews individuals involved with a problem and draws on their cognitive maps the factors relating to and influencing the situation subsumed in the problem. A single person might indicate tens of factors relating to a particular problem. The facilitator constructs a COPE model to reflect a person's view. The group as a whole can express thousands of views and COPE is designed to accumulate and compress this diversity of ideas.

COPE has been used to help identify resistance in implementing ideas (see Bessant and Buckingham 1989). InfoMap Lite also offers the possibility of being useful at this stage in the process since it enables one to map the points of view of different groups of people (see Figure 12.8). By showing groups their own and other's perspectives on an issue it is often possible to ease problems encountered in implementation.

Providing a smooth-running schedule with which to implement an idea and also being able to show to all concerned how the schedule is progressing are viewed as important. Computer software can make a major impact here and scheduling programs such as Symantec's Time Line for Windows provide a good example.

Conclusion

There is a growing amount of software coming on to the market which is intended to assist the creative problem-solving process. Most of these packages assist in the process in one way or another and some aid people to move through the stages of creative problem solving. The emphasis so far appears to have been primarily on idea generation rather than on problem definition and evaluation of ideas. Clearly, there is a need to produce computer software that can be used at all three stages of creative problem solving.

There is a lack of data on how helpful all these programs are. Few studies have been undertaken to assess the value of computer aided creativity. There are certain potential pitfalls to using computer assisted creativity and these are related to inadvertently fettering creativity through negatively influencing natural thinking and social interaction processes. The availability of software support may lessen exchanges between people and replace it with more solitary and intellectually incestuous individual computer interaction. The beginner may have less opportunity to interact with the expert and acquire knowledge in this way. Moreover, experts may have less opportunity to interact with other experts who can evaluate their own thinking. For all users there is also the problem of the reinforcement of existing tendencies to miscategorize the nature of some problems.

References

Bar, J. (1989) 'A systematic technique for new product idea generation – the external brain', *R&D Management*, January, **1**, 20–9.

Bessant, J. and Buckingham, J. (1989) 'Organisational Learning for effective implementation of computer aided production', *Management, Creativity and Innovation Yearbook*, 2.

BRAIN (1985) T. Proctor, Management Dept, Keele University, Keele.

Brainbox, c/o Peter Smee, 33 Churchill Way, Peverell, Plymouth, PL3 4PS.

Brainstorm, (1982) Brainstorm Software Ltd, Ruislip, Middlesex, UK.

BRIAN (1985) M. Brown and D. A. Kolb, Sound Training, London.

COPE, Bath Software Research, University of Bath.

'Global Think Tank' and 'Operation Brainstorm', Robert L. A. Trost, CCI Ltd, PO Box 286, 6800 AG, Arnhem-NL, Holland.

IdeaFisher, Software Paradise Training Technology International, Reading.

Idea Generator Plus, Experience in Software, 200 Hearst Avenue, Berkeley, California, CA 94709, USA.

Idea Tree (1988) Mountain House Publishing, Waitsfield, Vermont, USA.

InfoMap Lite, CoCo Systems Ltd, 2 Mortens Wood, Amersham, Bucks, HP7 9EQ.

Kelly, G. (1955) *The Psychology of Personal Constructs: A Theory of Personality*, New York: Norton.

Lotus Notes, Lotus Development Corporation, Cambridge, MA, USA.

Maslow, A. H. (1954) *Motivation and Personality*, New York: Harper & Row.

MicroSaint, Micro Analysis and Design, Simulation Software Inc., 4900 Pearl East Circle, Suite 201E, Boulder, CO 80301.

MindLink Problem Solver, MindLink Inc., Box 247, North Pomfret, Vermont, VT 05053, USA.

MoonLite and BizIdea, Robert L. A. Trost, CCI Ltd, PO Box 286, 6800, AG Arnhem-NL, Holland.

OptionFinder, Option Technologies Ltd, Winchfield, Hants, UK.

Powersim, Modell Data AS, Helland, 5120 Manger, Norway.

Proctor, R. A. (1989) 'Innovations in new product screening and evaluation', *Technology Analysis and Strategic Management*, **1**, 313–23.

Rogers, C. (1954) 'Towards a theory of creativity', *Review of General Semantics*, **11**, 249–60.

Rokeach, M. (1979) *Understanding Human Values: Individual and Societal*, New York: The Free Press.

Shaw, M. L. (1982) 'PLANET: some experience in creating an integrated system for Repertory Grid applications on a microcomputer', *International Journal of Man–Machine Studies*, **17**, 345–60.

Simon, H. A. (1985) 'What we know about the creative process', in R. L. Kuhn (ed.), *Frontiers in Creative and Innovative Management*, New York: Ballinger.

TeamFocus, J. Nunamaker, University of Arizona, Tucson, AZ, USA.

The Solution Machine, The Gemini Group, R.D. 2, Box 117, Bedford, New York, NY 10506, USA.

Thunder Thought, T. A. Easton and R. West, R. K. West Consulting, PO Box 8059, Mission Hills, CA 91346, USA.

Time Line for Windows, SYMANTEC, 10201 Torre Avenue, Cupertino, CA 95014, USA.

UDECIDE, Steve Estvanik, Cascoly Software, 4528 36th NE, Seattle, WA 98105, USA.

VisionQuest, Collaborative Technologies Corporation, Austin, Texas, USA.

WEB (1989) Octave Associates Ltd, Alton, Hampshire, UK.

Young, L. W. (1989) *Decision Support and Idea Processing Systems*, Dubuque: W. C. Brown.

Further reading

Bransford, J. D. and Stein, B. S. (1993) *The Ideal Problem Solver*, New York: Freeman.

De Bono, E. (1970) *Lateral Thinking: Creativity Step by Step*, New York: Harper & Row.

Henry, J. (1991) *Creative Management*, London: Sage.

Hicks, M. J. (1991) *Problem Solving in Business and Management*, London: Chapman & Hall.

Kuhn, R. L. (ed.) (1988) *Handbook for Creative and Innovative Managers*, New York: McGraw-Hill, pp. 77–89.

Majaro, S. (1991) *The Creative Marketer*, Oxford: Butterworth Heinemann.

Majaro, S. (1992a) *Strategy Search and Creativity: the Key to Corporate Renewal*, Maidenhead: McGraw-Hill.

Majaro, S. (1992b) *Managing Ideas for Profit*, Maidenhead: McGraw-Hill.

Rickards, T. (1990) *Creativity and Problem Solving at Work*, Aldershot: Gower.

Schon, D. A. (1991) *The Reflective Practitioner: How Professionals Think in Action*, Aldershot: Avebury.

Sternberg, R. J. (ed.) (1988) *The Nature of Creativity*, New York: Cambridge University Press.

Van Gundy, A. B. (1988) *Techniques of Structured Problem Solving*, New York: Van Nostrand Reinhold.

Van Gundy, A. B. (1992) *Idea Power*, New York: American Management Association.

Young, L. W. (1989) *Decision Support and Idea Processing Systems*, Dubuque: W. C. Brown.

Index